Praise for *Data-Driven Decisions*

'If the thought of data collection and analysis fills you with dread, then in under 200 pages this book will give you the confidence to forge ahead with a simple-to-use step-by-step toolkit. Written in an easy-to-follow conversational style, Stubbing's almost personal approach – even factoring in tea and coffee breaks! – offers clear instructions from identifying your data needs, and collecting, mapping, and analysing data results, to writing compelling reports to share with peers, senior colleagues and the LIS sector. In a world where the need for data analytics is growing exponentially, I highly recommend this book, tackling what can be a complex area, in a light hearted yet engaging way.'
Marilyn Clarke, Director of Library Services, Goldsmiths, University of London

'*Data-Driven Decisions* is a warm, friendly and accessible guide to using data in libraries. Amy has managed to shine a light on the monster that is 'data', and it turns out it isn't as scary as it's made out to be! Through the toolkit, each stage of the process is unpicked, examples shared and tips given freely. The answers aren't always easy, but Amy writes as your experienced colleague nudging you in the right direction and helping you along with way, with some cautionary tales to help you avoid learning the hard way! With examples that many in the library and information world will immediately recognise, the reader is empowered to work through their own data questions from the very start; from considering the design and purpose of the data and framing the data query, through to presenting and most importantly, taking action with what the data has shared. The voices of experience included lend a further dimension, giving real-life examples of the advice and best practice in action. These case studies shed a light on how data supports all aspects of our work, and how data can be found in all sorts of places. This is a generous book that will encourage all who try it out to make their data work harder for them.'
Catherine Stephen, Deputy Director Collections at Senate House Library, University of London

'Amy Stubbing has provided a clear and concise toolkit for data-driven decision making. Not only is the approach enjoyable, it brings to life the art of using data effectively. She takes the reader step-by-step from collecting and management of data to analysis, action and implementation. Amy transforms complexity into a joy to read. She helps the novice to gain confidence and to fend off any fear of data deluge. Leo Appleton's essay on data derived from social media complements Amy's text perfectly. Both reach beyond libraries to many other services.'

John Tuck, former Director of Library Services, Royal Holloway, University of London (2008–19) and Interim Director of Senate House Library (2019–20)

Data-Driven Decisions

Every purchase of a Facet book helps to fund
CILIP's advocacy, awareness and accreditation programmes
for information professionals.

Data-Driven Decisions

A Practical Toolkit for Library and Information Professionals

Amy Stubbing

© Chapters 1–8 & 10 Amy Stubbing 2022
© Chapters 9 & 11–14: the Contributors 2022

Published by Facet Publishing
c/o British Library, 96 Euston Road, London NW1 2DB
www.facetpublishing.co.uk

Facet Publishing is wholly owned by CILIP: the Library and Information Association.

The editor and authors of the individual chapters assert their moral right to be identified as such in accordance with the terms of the Copyright, Designs and Patents Act 1988.

Except as otherwise permitted under the Copyright, Designs and Patents Act 1988 this publication may only be reproduced, stored or transmitted in any form or by any means, with the prior permission of the publisher, or, in the case of reprographic reproduction, in accordance with the terms of a licence issued by The Copyright Licensing Agency. Enquiries concerning reproduction outside those terms should be sent to Facet Publishing, c/o British Library, 96 Euston Road, London NW1 2DB.

Every effort has been made to contact the holders of copyright material reproduced in this text, and thanks are due to them for permission to reproduce the material indicated. If there are any queries please contact the publisher.

British Library Cataloguing in Publication Data
A catalogue record for this book is available from the British Library.

ISBN 978-1-78330-478-3 (paperback)
ISBN 978-1-78330-479-0 (hardback)
ISBN 978-1-78330-480-6 (PDF)
ISBN 978-1-78330-522-3 (EPUB)

First published 2022

Typeset from authors' files in 10/13pt Palatino Linotype and Myriad Pro by Flagholme Publishing Services.
Printed and made in Great Britain by CPI Group (UK) Ltd, Croydon, CR0 4YY.

For Dominique – there's no metric that could show just how much I love you.

Contents

Figures and Tables	**xiii**
Contributors	**xv**
Acknowledgements	**xvii**
PART 1 BACKGROUND	**1**
1 Introduction	**3**
About the author	3
The wider context	4
The what, the why and the where of the data-driven decision process	6
The toolkit?	7
Going further	8
What will you get from this book?	8
2 Using the Toolkit	**9**
Getting started	9
Book layout	9
The model	10
A circular approach	11
PART 2 THE TOOLKIT	**13**
3 Step 1: Identify	**15**
Introduction	15
Data needs	15
Data queries	16
Data sources	17
Time to practise	21
Summary	22

x DATA-DRIVEN DECISIONS

4 Step 2: Collect **23**
Introduction 23
Choosing your data 23
Data collection methods 26
Summary 38

5 Step 3: Map **39**
Introduction 39
What is mapping? 39
Making data comparable (normalising) 40
Visualisation 48
Creating a map of your data 52
Summary 55

6 Step 4: Analyse **57**
Introduction 57
What is analysis? 57
Understand context 60
Conclusions 62
Summary 68

7 Step 5: Act **69**
Introduction 69
What is the action step? 69
Sharing data 70
Planning actions 73
Summary 75

8 Step 6: Review **77**
Introduction 77
Why do we review? 77
What do we review? 78
How to review and questions to explore 78
Make the changes 80
What next? 82

PART 3 GOING FURTHER **83**
9 Moving from a Transactional to a Transformational Service Using Data **85**
  Helen Rimmer
Introduction 85
Why lead with data? 85
Transactional vs transformational work 86
Data-led culture 86
Data with compassion 89
Case study 90

CONTENTS xi

10 Collection Mapping for Collection Management 97
Amy Stubbing
Introduction 97
Understanding your collection as a concept 97
Collection mapping 98
Conclusion 106

11 User Experience and Qualitative Data 107
Emilia Brzozowska-Szczecina
Introduction 107
What is UX? 107
Undertaking UX research in a library 108
The UX techniques 108
Ethics of research 117
Recruiting participants 118
Analysis 119
Now write it up! 122
What next? 123
Words of caution 125
This is the beginning 125

12 Alternative Data Sources: Using Digital and Social Media to Inform 127
Management Decisions in Your Library
Leo Appleton
Introduction 127
Libraries and social media 128
Social media terminology and background 129
What sort of data are we talking about? 129
Data from social media marketing activity 130
User engagement data and dialogue (outcomes measurement and evaluation) 134
Service improvements and customer services 135
Altmetrics 136
Web-based analytics 137
Summary 140

13 Starting from Scratch: Building a Data Culture at the University of 141
Westminster
Sarah Maule
Background 141
Overnight opening case study 143
Lessons learned and reflection 152

xii   DATA-DRIVEN DECISIONS

**14   Back to the Drawing Board: How Data Visualisation Techniques Informed   155
Service Delivery during the COVID-19 Pandemic**
   Elaine Sykes
   Setting the scene   155
   Background   156
   Piktochart   156
   Power BI   158
   Case study: the pandemic   159
   Final thoughts   164

Appendix   169

Bibliography   171

Index   175

Figures and Tables

Figures

2.1	The data-driven decision making model	11
5.1	Daily book loans and monthly gate count, May 2017; an example of poorly mapped data which hasn't been normalised	42
5.2	Daily book loans and monthly gate count, May 2017; an example of poorly mapped data which has been normalised	42
5.3	Monthly loans and gate count, 2017; an example of normalised and mapped data	43
5.4	Daily loans and gate count, 2017; an example of normalised and mapped data	43
5.5	Loans by day of week; an example of misleading data	50
5.6	Average headcount by area and hourly loans; an example of poorly mapped data from multiple data sources	51
5.7	Loans compared with items in repository (by Dewey) and new orders; an example of mapped data from three data sources	52
5.8	Data map showing how the number of activities changed in a public library when a new events post was created	54
6.1	Unnamed trends over three years	64
6.2	Live chat enquiries over five years	65
6.3	Average shelving time for one trolley (October Year 1 to April Year 2); an example of normalised and mapped data	67
7.1	Example of a Gantt chart	75
10.1	Undergraduate and postgraduate classical civilisations loans by Dewey area	104
11.1	Observations made daily for a week at 11 a.m. in the silent study area of Kingston Hill Library, Kingston University London	113
12.1	The marketing cycle	131
13.1	Average occupancy at 1 a.m. at all UoW library sites	148
13.2	Percentage capacity at different UoW library sites at 1 a.m.	149
14.1	Excerpt from a Faculty NSS report (using sample data) showing levels of satisfaction with library services divided into 'investigate' and 'celebrate' categories	157

xiv   DATA-DRIVEN DECISIONS

| 14.2 | The VLOOKUP function in Excel | 160 |
| 14.3 | First draft of an activity dashboard for case study | 163 |

Tables

3.1	Examples of data sources and their data type	20
3.2	Example of data needs and related data queries and data sources	21
4.1	Benefits and drawbacks to short and long periods of data collection	25
4.2	The type of picture you can gain from different periods of data collection	25
4.3	Data needs and related data queries, data sources, time frames and frequency of data collection	27
4.4	Manual data collection plan for a university library	29
4.5	Example of a poorly laid out spreadsheet	31
4.6	Headcount of occupancy of library, 1–14 January 2020, by level and time; example of a well laid out spreadsheet	33
4.7	Headcount of occupancy of library, 1–14 January 2020, by level and time, with daily totals	34
5.1	Example of qualitative data translated into themes: the subjects of feedback postcards in September	48
6.1	Example figures for calculating a mean average	58
9.1	Breakdown of data collected by five liaison librarians in case study	91
9.2	Breakdown of data collected in case study showing highest statistics in six subjects	92
9.3	Tasks the liaison team spent most of their time on in case study, by broad area	93
9.4	Time liaison librarians spent on 'non-core' tasks each week in case study	94
9.5	Highest amount of time liaison librarians spent on tasks in case study, by category	95
10.1	Subject areas of a university library mapped to the corresponding Dewey area	103
10.2	How three criteria for individual titles fit into the four categories flagship, heritage, current and finite	106
11.1	Elements of the FRAMES model set out as a table, adapted from Campbell Galman (2016)	123
12.1	Framework that measures web impact through internal and external data on user behaviour and user traces	138
13.1	The original evening opening hours at the four sites of the UoW, semesters 1 and 2, academic year 2017/18	143
13.2	Data types and data gained from various sources for this case study	144
13.3	Hourly headcounts at Harrow Library, 23 September to 8 October 2013; an example of a poorly laid out spreadsheet	145
13.4	Hourly headcounts at Cavendish Library, two weeks of autumn term 2014/15; an example of a well laid out spreadsheet	146

Contributors

The author

Amy Stubbing has had a varied career across different sectors in the library and information profession. She is currently the Academic Engagement Lead at the University of Westminster where she is responsible for strategic planning and the development of the learning support provision for the university, including academic liaison, academic learning development, and specific learning difficulty/disability support. Previous roles include Campus Library Manager at the University of East London, and the Library Customer Care Collections Coordinator at Royal Holloway University.

Amy's interest in data and using it to inform service decisions and developments to improve user experience has been a core part of her career. She has a particular passion for developing data literacy and embedding data practices into all decision making, which led to her developing her Data-Driven Decisions toolkit for libraries. She has worked with numerous university libraries to begin working towards embedding a culture of data-driven decisions, and has used her varied experience of teaching data literacy to further develop her toolkit, culminating in this book.

The contributors

Leo Appleton

Leo Appleton is a senior university teacher in the Information School at the University of Sheffield. He teaches about many aspects of library and information service management and has many years' experience of managing academic libraries. He has published and presented on many topics during his career, including the value of public libraries, performance measurement, library space design and how libraries use social media.

Emilia Brzozowska-Szczecina

Emilia works as a senior information adviser for economics and business-related subjects at Kingston University London. She holds master's degrees in Library and Information Science and Polish Literature with Anthropology. Emilia is very passionate about user experience research and delivering information literacy training in a fun and engaging way.

Sarah Maule

Sarah is Planning and Development Lead at the University of Westminster. Her professional interests include material libraries, managing libraries for art and design courses, staff development and ensuring libraries are collecting the right data to inform their services.

Helen Rimmer

Helen Rimmer is Head of Library and Archives Service at the University of Westminster, having previously held roles at different levels at Royal Holloway, City University, INTO UEA (a partnership between INTO and the University of East Anglia) and the University of Brighton. She is passionate about compassionate leadership, data-driven management and flexible working.

Elaine Sykes

Elaine Sykes is Head of Open Research at Lancaster University and was previously Team Leader (Business Control) at Liverpool John Moores University. Outside work she is kept entertained by her two-year-old twin girls. When time and twins allow, she enjoys baking, reading and playing the violin in a local orchestra.

Acknowledgements

This book was in many ways a labour of love, and without the expertise, time and support of a number of people would not have been possible.

First thanks goes to my excellent contributors, who gave up their time and brain space in the middle of a global pandemic. These wonderful humans have navigated writing through intense workloads, illness, changes to bed-time routines, welcoming newborn babies into their lives and growing tiny humans. Their input has made this much more than a 'how to' guide, and I'm so grateful that they have been willing to share their knowledge and experiences in this book.

Huge credit also goes to Pete Baker at Facet, who has had endless patience with me throughout this process, and who has been an incredible help and support while getting this book finished.

Next I thank Sean O'Donohoe and Helen Rimmer, both of whom helped me develop a pipe dream into a real plan and vision for a book.

Special mention also goes to my long suffering but loyal friends who have listened to me talk about this project for far too long, have cast fresh eyes over chapters and data, and helped me through this entire process.

Finally, I am most thankful to my husband, James. Through endless projects, volunteering and extra curriculars he has given me unwavering support. He's read this book more times than anyone else, proofed chapters, helped draft figures, and built me up when I have very much needed it. Without him, this book wouldn't exist.

PART 1
Background

1 Introduction

Well hello there! Welcome to my little book about all things data. Delightful to have you here.

I can assume that the fact that you have begun this introductory chapter means one of three things:

- You love data and you will read any book which covers the topic.
- You don't love data but appreciate the need to learn more about it.
- You picked this up by accident and are now regretting your choice.

Whatever your reason for picking up this tome today, I hope it allows you to love and use data a little bit more than you did before.

About the author

It feels uncomfortable to start with a section about myself, but as you will find out when you delve further into this book, *context is everything,* and I'm not about to deprive you of it here!

If you had asked me ten years ago what I would spend most of my time learning and discussing in my career, I can guarantee that data would not have come anywhere near the top of the list. I was never bad at maths, but I was never in love with it. I loved the arts and reading, and I dropped subjects like maths and science as soon as possible to pursue more theatrical endeavours. This culminated in me taking a degree in Music and English where the maths and statistics part of my brain was left to gather dust.

In the early days of my career, I spent most of my time working with charities to improve the care system and the support offered to children in care and care leavers (like myself). My experiences working with the care

4 DATA-DRIVEN DECISIONS

system were formative in my decision to move into libraries for my career. I started working in libraries because I believe that they are a great equaliser, and that libraries can be the difference between someone succeeding in their goals and not having the opportunity to even try. There were also other more surprising takeaways which have stuck with me and influenced my approaches.

After my graduate traineeship at the London Library, my first full-time professional post in the information profession was at a private school library. I naively thought that because the school was so well funded and the library so well presented, we wouldn't have to fight to be seen as relevant, or for funding, or to be used appropriately. It will come as no surprise to you that I very quickly realised that this school library (like many) was undervalued and misunderstood, and because of this we were not able to support the number of students we should in the way we could.

This was the moment my background working (and living) in the care system kicked into action. When working in charities, or in any underfunded body, fighting to be seen, understood and supported is a core part of the gig. How do we do this? First we shout loudly, and second we know how to evidence our value. That's what I did in this role – I collected data, wrote reports, made changes to our service based on the data, and then wrote more reports. Thus a data lover was born.

Using evidence to make decisions and prove value followed me through my transition into higher education and in every role I've held in the information profession.

The wider context

Now we're done with my life story, let's look at the current context in the information profession, which has spawned the need for this book.

To say that it has been a difficult few decades for the library and information profession might be one of the biggest understatements I could make. In the last three decades the UK and the USA have had three major recessions: the early 1990s recession, the Great Recession and, finally, the COVID-19 recession (Investopedia, 2021). Alongside recurrent financial instability, we've also seen the digital revolution, which has had a significant impact on how library and information services are used, what services we offer, and what our role is within wider institutions.

With the various recessions and the digital revolution, library and information services have naturally faced increasing financial challenges. Across the sector we have seen services closed, restructures which have

INTRODUCTION 5

significantly reduced staff numbers, and cuts to resourcing budgets, to name a few. On top of this we're seeing already restricted budgets challenged with increased costs of key resources such as online materials, or the need for additional resources to keep up with the changing needs of our users and organisations. As well as various financial difficulties our sector is also having continuously to develop roles, services and our offer to remain relevant.

Naturally we can't fail to mention the COVID-19 pandemic, where regardless of skills, funds or nature, information professionals pivoted overnight to provide fully online services. The work done by libraries over this period has been nothing short of exceptional, but what does it mean for us moving forward? It is highly unlikely that the expectations born from COVID-19 and online services will go away, and instead we will work with a shift in needs of offline services alongside a continued increase in use of online services. Essentially, when coming out of a global recession, library services will need to redesign two services to work in harmony, both of which will likely have increased usage and costs over the previous model.

That's a lot for one sector to be dealing with over 30 years, right?

What do we do about it?
We can't change the global situation, and we aren't going to be able to predict or stop future recessions, pandemics or revolutions. What we can do, though, is prepare, stay ahead of the curve, and make our services as effective, innovative and relevant as possible.

Arguably the factor that most impacts library and information services right now is financial scrutiny, which may lead to cuts in services and budgets, freezes in budgets, or much more difficulty in getting increases in budgets for new developments. This continued (and in many cases increased) financial difficulty means that:

- services that are not working as effectively and efficiently as possible are more likely to be scrutinised
- services need to be creative to find resources within current means to continue developing
- staff need to be able to articulate and prove the value and impact of services to protect them against cuts and argue for additional funds.

But how do we do this? Well my friend, considering you picked up this book it won't surprise you to know that in my humble opinion, *data is the answer*.

The what, the why and the where of the data-driven decision process

Why data-driven decisions?

Data-driven decision making is a well-developed concept with a huge amount of literature on the subject focusing across professions. At its core, data-driven decision making is about being data informed and using your understanding of data to feed into all aspects of your decision making and planning. If we are able to commit to data-driven decision making we can:

- examine our services to ensure they are effective and efficient
- identify areas for improvement or areas of success which can be replicated
- identify changing needs and trends in order to develop new services and strategies around them
- articulate our strengths as a service and the importance of maintaining it.

Considering the context outlined above, it has never been more important for library and information services staff to be able to harness and use data for decision making. Our services are transformative. They make a difference to people's lives, to research, to learning. If we are not able to commit to new ways of developing our services and working within the language and needs of decision makers in our organisations (using data), our services will always be at risk.

A toolkit is born

Although I did not come up with the concept of data-driven decision making, in this book I have aimed to make the act (and art) of data-driven decision making more accessible. The way that data is tied up with science, maths and technology, and the need to be able to use systems in new ways, can make it complicated and scary for many people to understand and use data. In my experience this is particularly prevalent in librarianship where using data to its fullest potential and making better use of technology has been slower than in other industries. There are such varied backgrounds and routes into the industry that confidence or experience in using data and technology is not guaranteed and data and digital literacy levels among staff can vary massively.

As my experience and love for data grew I wanted to get data usage and data-driven decision making embedded across my team and across my library service. Naturally I quickly hit a wall where my colleagues and staff just weren't comfortable or confident enough to take an active role in the work that I was suggesting. I had an uphill battle to explain and help them to understand why we needed data. I'm a firm believer that you can learn anything with the right training, so I tried to find resources and programmes which I could use with my team. Unfortunately, everything I came across just didn't hit the right level or was so abstract that staff struggled to transfer the information to their own real-life needs.

It was clear to me that there was a gap in quality training materials available. From working with colleagues across the sector it was obvious that there was a need for a no-nonsense and accessible step-by-step guide to break down how to begin using data and how it can be used to improve services through informed decision making. This is essentially how the idea for the data-driven decisions toolkit came to be.

The toolkit

We are at the stage where we can address the elephant in the room – what is this toolkit?

The data-driven decisions toolkit is a simple, jargon free, step-by-step guide for understanding and implementing data collection and analysis for decision making in library services. It is designed to walk you through each stage of implementing and embedding data-driven decision making, filling in the gaps that a lot of training has, and putting it in the context of library and information services. The toolkit is designed to be used however you need, whether to follow the entire process from start to finish or dip into a specific subject, depending on what you are wanting to learn or refresh. It can also be used as a tool to consolidate data practices and create a common language for a team to work under.

How does this toolkit fill the gap?

Over the last few years the toolkit has taken a few iterations, moving from a talk to a downloadable mini toolkit, and finally into its current form – this book. It has developed and transformed as needs have changed and new needs have arisen.

The point of the toolkit is to make data and the data-driven decision process accessible to everyone. Unlike the other, more general, resources referenced above, this toolkit:

- frames data and data-driven decision making in the context of the information profession

8 DATA-DRIVEN DECISIONS

- transforms the process of making data-driven decisions into a step-by-step, followable guide
- makes no assumptions about the reader's previous skill levels and knowledge, allowing them to start from the beginning of using data
- offers a set approach and common language for entire teams and organisations to implement effective data-driven decisions
- allows readers to fill the gaps in their knowledge and jump to relevant aspects and information.

Going further

The final section of this book is entitled 'Going Further', where we will (unsurprisingly) be going past the toolkit and into using data-driven decision in practice. In this section, contributing authors will explore specific applications of data-driven decisions, from collection management to resource distribution, and even staffing. The section includes case studies where you will be able to explore experiences of using data in real life, how it can work great and how it can go wrong or be pulled into different directions as the world outside of the toolkit impacts our work, and how we can still succeed despite changes and setbacks. There are also chapters dedicated to specific areas of using data in a more complex and nuanced way, which you can explore when you've built up your confidence and want to get even more from data-driven decisions.

What will you get from this book?

When you have finished reading this book you will be confident enough about the fundamentals of data and using data for decision making to set up your own data-driven decision practices and projects. This book does not try to answer every single data question or teach absolutely everything you need to know about data, but it will give you a solid foundation on your data journey. I hope you enjoy reading as much as I have enjoyed putting this together.

2 Using the Toolkit

Getting started

How you use the toolkit is entirely up to you and will depend on what you need from the book. It has been designed so that you can use it as a manual to walk through each step for implementation, as an introduction and teaching resource for initial learning, and as a guide to refer to once data-driven decision practices are in place. As your skills and situations change, so can the way you use this book.

Although this toolkit can be used for one-off projects when you are in the early stages of learning and building data practices in your workplace, the emphasis and purpose of this book is to be able to develop *continued* data processes. Keep that in mind as you push through the next six chapters!

Book layout

What makes this book a bit different from other 'how to' style texts is that we will explore the toolkit and data-driven decision making in practice. The book is split into two main parts. In the first we start with the toolkit and walk you through all the big things you need to know to use data and commit to data-driven decision making. The second section takes you a step further, focusing instead on specific and more specialised topics for you to widen your understanding and approaches to making data-driven decisions, written by people who have lived and breathed data in practice. This second section will allow you to get real-life ideas for how you could use data-driven decisions, and will allow you to dive into areas of data and using data as and when you are feeling confident enough.

The idea of this book and the two parts is that the toolkit will first teach you, then support you as you live it, and the final section will give you the expertise and inspiration to develop your foundation of knowledge.

10 DATA-DRIVEN DECISIONS

A core feature of the book is that you can jump between the toolkit and the chapters in Part 3. You can choose to head to the chapters in Part 3 as you work on one area from the toolkit, or you can focus on the toolkit and read the other chapters at a later date as a focused look at data collection and analysis approaches. Equally, when you are at the stage of using this book as a reference for your practice you can dive into a specific area easily.

Chapter layout

At the start of each chapter there is a short introduction which lists what topics will be covered in each chapter, along with page numbers for you to whizz right to your designated topic if you are using the book as a reference guide. You can use these introductions to enable you to use the book as a quick reference guide once you are familiar with the toolkit.

> Alongside the main content there are additional tips and thoughts dotted throughout the toolkit in boxes that look like this. They give context to the key themes in the chapter.

Once you get into the main part of each chapter you will notice that content is broken into smaller, manageable topics, making it easy for you to start and stop your learning quickly and pick up and refresh specific areas without wading through the entire chapter.

As well as walking you through the key things you need to know about data and using data, the book has top tips and resources for getting your data-driven decisions approach into practice.

The model

What is this grand toolkit we've mentioned approximately 369 times in just two short chapters?

The toolkit centres on the model depicted in Figure 2.1. There are six distinct steps, which should be followed for every instance where you collect data or attempt to answer a question with data:

- *Step 1: Identify* your data need, query and source – everything you need to move forward with the toolkit.
- *Step 2: Collect*, store and prep your data for analysis.
- *Step 3: Map* your data to allow for more detailed analysis by creating visualisations, overlaying different types of data, and making your data comparable.

USING THE TOOLKIT 11

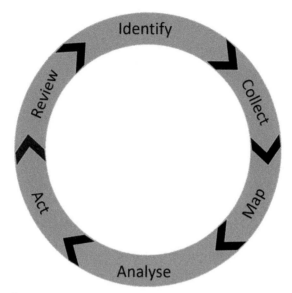

Figure 2.1 *The data-driven decision making model*

- *Step 4: Analyse* and draw conclusions from your data by identifying anomalies, using context to understand the data, and reviewing your visualisations.
- *Step 5: Act* on your data – plan and execute actions based on your understanding of it after going through steps 1 to 4.
- *Step 6: Review* all the work of the previous steps, looking at the data you have and carrying out process reviews and analysing procedures. Check if you have omitted anything.

A circular approach

The model doesn't end after Step 6. In embracing data-driven decision making we are not simply putting in place measures for single use. We are committing to creating a culture of using data continuously to shape our understanding and decision making. The ultimate goal of this toolkit is to create a rich and extensive tapestry of data which can be drawn on for decision making. The model never really ends. When you have reviewed your processes, you move right back to Step 1 and identify what data will fill the gaps you have highlighted from Step 6, and so the cycle continues.

PART 2
The Toolkit

PART 2

3 Step 1: Identify

Introduction

In this chapter we go right back to basics about using and understanding data. Our key goal by the end of this chapter is that you will be able to identify why you need data, what data you need, and where you can get that data from. To do this, we explore and learn about:

- data needs and queries (pages 15, 16)
- types of data (page 17)
- identifying data and planning how to use it (pages 17, 18)
- sources of data (page 19).

Data needs

Finding out your data need is a key part of learning how to use and understand data, and to progressing with this model. Essentially, it's really important, so read the next bit carefully.

Before we start looking at what types of data there are and how to choose what to explore, we need first to think about what we actually want the data for. One of the biggest crimes you can commit in data-driven decision making is to collect data with no purpose nor plan about how you can use it. To avoid said crime, always start your data-driven decision planning by *identifying* your data need.

What is a data need?

In the context of this book and model, a data need is simply what you are trying to achieve or do that requires data. More than anything, identifying

16 DATA-DRIVEN DECISIONS

your data needs is about being able to gain understanding so that you can then do something. One way of pinning down your data need is to answer the question 'Why do you need this data?'.

Identifying your data needs

Thinking about what you want to achieve can be difficult, particularly when you have not thought much about using data for service development in the past. There are, however, a few things you can do to start planning and identifying what you need to find out.

One of the easiest ways to start yourself off with identifying a data need is to think about what areas you know could do with improvement. Try to think of a specific one to look at that is relatively top level and based on a specific problem or thing you want to achieve. Your data need might relate to:

- reporting on your value as a service
- improving your staffing efficiency
- developing your shelving processes to be more efficient
- improving user experience in a specific area
- ensuring you have the right items in your collection.

These are broad goals, and it might feel difficult to know where to start. Indeed, not everything is going to translate to easily collectable data, but we will explore how to manage complicated data needs in later chapters. The most important thing right now is that you can pull on different areas that you want to understand.

As well as focusing on areas for improvement, look at what you already think is going well. Exploring both areas will help you to look at what is working or not working and why, and enable you to emulate successes in other areas through this understanding.

When thinking about what your data needs might be, flick to Table A.1 in the appendix (or download it onto your computer) and write some of them down.

Data queries

Your data query is the next piece in the puzzle – all the individual questions which will enable you to address your data need. While your data need is a top level or overarching goal you wish to achieve, your data query will comprise specific questions, such as:

- 'What is the headcount data on each floor?'
- 'What times are people borrowing and returning books?'
- 'How many enquiries are we receiving?'

Sometimes you will have a very specific need for your data which would essentially mirror your data query. That's absolutely fine and will be common when you are first exploring data. However, as you build up your knowledge, confidence and the pool of data you have available, you will begin noticing that the type of data needs you are identifying will become more complicated and nuanced.

Data sources

Types of data

Once you have identified your data need and data queries the next thing to think about is your data source: what data will answer your query. Before we think about how you can identify your data sources, we need to roll back to basics and have a quick look at what different types of data there are.

We will look at the two key categories of data types – quantitative and qualitative – and what each might be useful for. We will go into more detail about analysing them in later chapters.

Quantitative data – numbers and more numbers

At the most basic description, quantitative data is data in numbers. It is often collected automatically in your different online systems. For example, in a library management system (LMS), the total number of loans are quantitative data. You can manually collect quantitative data, for example, data on headcounts, enquiry numbers and so on, which we will come to a little later.

To gain a real understanding of quantitative data, and to be able to use it to answer your data need, you require large quantities of data or to have gathered data over long periods of time. In many ways, it is easier to analyse quantitative data than qualitative data as it does not require further categorisation or individual exploration of data entries, so it is a good place to start exploring your analysis techniques. The great thing about quantitative data is that it is much easier to visualise the data in graphs and to illustrate what the situation in the area of concern is. This naturally makes it easier to understand what is going on. It also tends to be easier to overlay and cross-analyse quantitative data (depending on the level of granularity you

18 DATA-DRIVEN DECISIONS

have available – see Chapter 4), which can really help you to draw more valuable conclusions from your data (to come in Chapter 5).

To sum up, quantitative data is big, numerical and your friend in the wide world of data analysis.

Qualitative data – words and types

I won't lie to you, I started you off with quantitative data as it is much easier to pin down and describe than qualitative data, which in a lot of ways is the opposite of quantitative data. While we will do some work later on in this book to combine the two, for now it might help you to think of them as separate entities.

While quantitative data is all about numbers, qualitative data focuses on words, types and categories. Unlike quantitative data, we often use qualitative data in an investigative manner, so responses and data gathered are often generated after asking open-ended questions or arise from situations where we are not restricting the potential responses. For example, responses and insights gained from an interview or focus group are qualitative data. When using these techniques we are gaining much more detailed information but usually at a smaller scale than quantitative data. By its nature, therefore, qualitative data tends to have smaller sample sizes than quantitative data and is not often used for the ongoing understanding you may gain from quantitative data such as trends of library usage.

Qualitative data includes data on characteristics at an individual level. For example, user numbers, unique identifiers, sex and gender identity are all considered qualitative data.

Qualitative data requires a significantly different analysis approach than quantitative data. To analyse qualitative data you need to be able to understand the data on its own and to translate your data to make it comparable. See Chapter 5.

A mix of the two?

But what about when the categorical data is used in a quantitative way? There are naturally some grey areas and instances where data can be a mix of qualitative and quantitative. For example, let's look at the gender identity data again. On an individual level this is indeed qualitative data (the fact that it is categorised makes it inherently so), however if we look on a large scale at what percentage of users identify as female the figures would also be quantitative data.

Another example of data which skirts that line between qualitative and quantitative is data collected on a sliding scale. If we want to know whether a user's experience was poor, average or good we'd be collecting qualitative data, as this is categorical. However, it is also quantitative as we can analyse the data in a numerical way.

These distinctions and understandings are going to be really important, particularly when we look at how we combine data to get more in-depth analyses, so maybe pop a bookmark or sticky note on this page and reread it again after a strong cup of coffee.

Identifying your data source

Your data source is what data you need to answer your data query. Could I have just asked 'What source is your data going to come from?' Sure, but isn't there a certain elegance to shaving it down to two words and following it up with a two-line explanation?

Identifying your data source relies heavily on your having identified and understood your data need and query. Deciding on your data need and query should always be your first steps in the journey of making data-driven decisions, and you shouldn't even be thinking about your data source if you haven't come up with a reason why you actually require the data. This is a pretty vital aspect of our approach to data-driven decision making in this book, and has an important role when progressing within the toolkit. While you can gain good insights from data you have collected without deciding why you are collecting it, in taking this approach you risk losing focus and making incorrect assumptions from the data. This approach can also lead you to fall into problematic habits, which can waste time and derail embedding data-driven decision making into your service.

The key to identifying your data source is to look at your data query. When you are sure of your data query examine it and list what specific data will enable you to answer that query fully. In some instances, your data source will be clearly defined in your data query, which will make this stage of the step much easier (e.g. a query looking at how many loans there have been in a certain area needs loan statistics). In other cases, identifying the data source is less obvious and depending on the query it may even need multiple data sources. The more specific you are at this step the easier Step 2 of the toolkit is, so give it a good amount of time! This is probably one of the most difficult tasks to learn to do in this process, but once you have got the hang of it, it will become second nature.

20   DATA-DRIVEN DECISIONS

You may already have data collection processes in place, but when identifying your data source you need to imagine you know nothing about what data you have already, how you collect it or how you use it. It can be difficult to step away from what you know your different data situations and perceived limitations are. When identifying your data source, you must look at your data query with as fresh eyes as possible. This is important because if you follow the same assumptions and ways of working you have had before, you will very easily fall into the trap of collecting data that doesn't fully answer your query, or worse – modifying your query to fit the data. Unlearning a way of thinking or doing can be tough. This is not easy to teach, it is not easy to learn, but you still need to commit to a fresh eye approach every time you start this process.

Some tips for committing to a fresh eye approach:

- Ask a colleague from a different team or organisation what their immediate thoughts are on your data query.
- Formulate a plan, sleep on it and review it the next day.
- Start with things you know you haven't got right or need improvement.
- Have a cup of tea. Tea helps everything.

This is not to say that what you may already know or have in place is wrong, but be prepared to question why this is the best option over a different approach, and what the reasoning is for any current approaches you have in place.

It can be a challenge to think about where you can get your data from, especially when you are just starting your data journey. Table 3.1 shows some examples of data sources with their data type.

Table 3.1 *Examples of data sources and their data type*

Data source	Data type
Headcount and space usage statistics	Quantitative
Item usage (in-house and regular loans)	Quantitative
Loan and return times	Quantitative
Time from return to on shelf	Quantitative
Usage of specific user types	Quantitative
Type of queries	Qualitative
Number of queries	Quantitative
Complaints	Qualitative
User feedback	Qualitative and quantitative
Staff task distribution	Quantitative
Total visitors	Quantitative
Teaching, activity, session engagement	Qualitative
User experience work	Blended

STEP 1: IDENTIFY   21

Time to practise

Table A.1 in the appendix helps you map out your data needs and collection phases. Use it initially to get used to mapping out needs, queries and sources; once you are more confident, use it to identify overlapping data needs and how your processes can be more efficient (discussed in Chapter 4).

> Naturally everyone using this book or considering beginning making data-driven decisions will have access to different sources of data and need different data to enable them to make data-driven decisions, but these broad areas should get the brain juices flowing and help you with the final section of this chapter.

We don't want to jump ahead too far, so will start by focusing on the first three columns of Table A.1.

Table 3.2 gives two examples of data needs, with their related data queries and data sources. This is just one way that these data needs could be mapped; you might come up with different queries and sources for these data needs – and that's okay! Data-driven decision making really is a creative act and no two people's processes will look exactly the same. As your experience and confidence grows you will likely come up with different things to fill in on the table. It's all part of the continuous learning process.

Table 3.2 *Example of data needs and related data queries and data sources*

Data need	Data query	Data source
Developing our library spaces in line with user needs	'How are students using the space currently?' 'What do students want from their study spaces?' 'What are the top enquiries relating to library spaces?'	Headcount User experience In-house loans User experience Surveys Enquiries – most common and related to spaces Space-related enquiries
Improving our staffing efficiencies	'When are users using the enquiry desk?' 'When are users borrowing and returning books?' 'When are users using the spaces?' 'What enquiries are we receiving?'	Number and time of enquiries Borrowing and return – location of items, time Headcount Time of borrowing and return Type and number of enquiries Complaints

Filling in the table yourself – a quick reminder

In Column 1 write down exactly what you want to understand. This is a top-level reflection on what you are trying to do by collecting and analysing your data, which will enable you to focus on your specific data query. This

22   DATA-DRIVEN DECISIONS

could be reviewing library staffing levels, developing the library space, decision making for purchasing and weeding, and so on. The key here is to make sure that you are describing an action or purpose rather than just the specific information you are trying to collect.

In Column 2 think about what data query to explore to help you meet goals you listed in Column 1. To start, try and think of specific queries or answers you hope to gain which will enable you to complete your action from Column 1. For example, if my data need (the action which I am going to undertake) is to review staffing levels throughout the day, I may want to look at what library usage is like at different times of the day. Equally, if I'm planning to weed a collection, I may need to find out what items have not been borrowed in a certain time frame. Note that your data need from Column 1 may have multiple data queries, which you can set out in this table.

Now you have your action and query planned out, in Column 3 identify the different sources of data which will answer your data query. Don't forget to try and approach this with the fresh eye we discussed earlier. Think outside the box and really try and come up with exactly what data would answer your query. You may need more than one piece of data, and often the data need for one query is the same as for another query, which is fine too!

Summary

Starting your data-driven decision process off the right way will have a huge impact on how well you can collect, analyse and understand your data. In a lot of ways good planning is the key takeaway in this toolkit, and if you have your foundations right then you have already won a major battle. You are learning a very specific way of thinking, and it takes a long time for that to be natural. It is worth revisiting this chapter over the course of your data journey, to refresh your understanding and gain new insights from your increased experience and confidence.

4 Step 2: Collect

Introduction

In this chapter we go through some background information on collection approaches as well as the key steps to beginning your data collection. By the end of this chapter you will be able to create and critically evaluate your data collection plan. To do this, we explore and learn about:

- how to choose data (page 23)
- data collection methods (page 26)
- evaluation methods (page 29)
- how to store and organise data (page 37).

Choosing your data

This might seem like an intimidating chapter to be heading into, but the beautiful thing about this whole step-by-step process is that you have already done the hard work for this bit. Huzzah for past you, huzzah for Chapter 3, and huzzah for data!

If you look back at Table 3.2, you will hopefully have a few examples of data sources to answer your data needs. The next step is to start planning some of the specifics about this data that you need to collect.

There are a few initial key questions to ask yourself when you begin planning your data collection:

- What timeframe (or period) does the data need to cover?
- How often do I need to collect this data?
- How granular does this data need to be?

24 DATA-DRIVEN DECISIONS

Timeframe

Making an active plan for your timeframe for collecting data is important to make sure you aren't wasting your time, and for planning your ongoing data-driven decision practices. Your timeframe for collecting this data could be two weeks, or you could collect this data forevermore. Whatever you decide, your current plan must support your future plans for making data-driven decisions and enable you to really understand what is happening from this data.

For example, if you choose to collect data for two weeks and then stop, be sure of what this information will actually be able to tell you. If you are collecting information on headcount numbers in a library building, two weeks' worth of data would show very different results depending on the time of year. Equally, there could be external factors during that two-week period which would give you a false understanding of the wider situation. Sometimes collecting data over a short period is appropriate, but be careful about how you then use the information from that data, and what decisions you might want to make from it. We will talk more about data analysis and assumptions in Chapter 6.

> It might be tempting to lean towards collecting data for less time. However, the shorter the period of data you end up analysing the more likely you are to make incorrect assumptions from this data. Equally, you might think that collecting loads of data forever is the answer, but you don't want to be collecting data for years if you are not going to actually use that data regularly or embed that data into a full data-driven decision plan. It's a nightmare tightrope you need to cross for every piece of data you start collecting, but it does get easier with practice.

To decide on your timeframe, first determine whether you need a snapshot to fulfil your data need or if you need a fuller understanding of the situation. If you need a snapshot, you will collect data for a shorter period; if you need a fuller understanding you will have to commit to collecting data for a longer time.

Table 4.1 opposite shows the benefits and drawbacks of collecting data for short and long timelines.

Sometimes you need a long period of data collection to achieve your data need and you might need to start from scratch in collecting this data. This is not uncommon, especially when you are first starting your journey of making data-driven decisions, and it can be frustrating to know it will take a long time to realise your goals. It's important to accept that you may not be able to answer your data query fully or achieve your data need with what you currently have or in a short period, but you can begin working towards these goals and gain an initial idea or picture. In these instances, keep in

STEP 2: COLLECT   25

Table 4.1   *Benefits and drawbacks to short and long periods of data collection*

Short periods of data collection	Long periods of data collection
Can give a brief snapshot of situation	Can give a much more reliable and nuanced picture
Should not be used for major decision making or broad assumptions on their own	Can be used to gain a broader understanding and for decision making
Useful when collecting qualitative data	Useful for quantitative (or translated qualitative) data
Can easily give a false picture and should be analysed in context	More likely to give a truer representation of the wider situation (considering different factors and contexts)
Useful when deciding and reviewing plans for larger data collection projects	More staff time required and commitment to collection
Good for in-depth studies such as user experience work	

mind the limitations of your data while making any initial analysis or decisions.

Once you have fully understood the limitations of your data, the final step to picking your timeframe is to answer this key question:

How much data will give me a real representation of what I need to know?

There is no magic formula to tell you the answer, but use Table 4.2 to give you an idea of the types of picture you can gain from different periods of data collection.

Table 4.2   *The type of picture you can gain from different periods of data collection*

Period of data collection	1–4 weeks	1–3 months	3 months to 1 year	Indefinite
Type of picture gained	Focused snapshot	Extended snapshot	Ongoing picture	Comparative and reflective picture

While looking at your timeframe for collecting data be aware of what the calendar looks like for your particular library type. Some libraries (such as university and school libraries) have distinct annual cycles, so making a direct comparison of data for less than two full cycles would likely give an unrealistic picture. For example, if you compared January loans with August loans to see the pattern of usage through the year you wouldn't gain a wide

26   DATA-DRIVEN DECISIONS

understanding on loan trends (for which you would need multiple years' worth of data from the same periods).

How often?

The next step is deciding how often you are going to collect your data:

- How many times a day, week, month or year will you collect the data?
- Decide how often to collect data within your data collection timeframe.
- How many times will you complete the cycle of collecting your data?
- When will you collect it – every day, Monday to Friday, one week in a month, one month in a year?

Deciding how often to collect your data will largely depend on your purpose for collecting it and your understanding of the specific needs and cycle of your organisation or situation. Whatever you decide, make sure that you take time to think about and discuss the implications of your choice with colleagues to ensure you can take any additional insights into account when using the data for understanding and decision making.

> A cautionary note: do not collect more data than you need. If you decide to collect data over long periods or continually, make sure you know why you are doing so, and how it will be used. Do not fall into the trap of collecting time exhaustive data every 2 hours, 24 hours a day, when you only really need to collect it every 4 hours for 18 hours of the day.
>
> Yes this is a real example. Yes it still keeps me awake at night.

Once you have decided your timeframe and how often you collect, you can add details to Table A.1.

Table 4.3 opposite shows a continued example from the information given in Table 3.2.

Do you see what we're doing? We're creating your data plan while you read this book. Easy peasy.

Data collection methods

Now you have thought about when and how often to collect data, we can move on to thinking about data collection methods: manual and automated. To move towards making data-driven decisions you need to use both. We will look at how we can bring them together in Chapter 5.

STEP 2: COLLECT   27

Table 4.3 *Data needs and related data queries, data sources, time frames and frequency of data collection*

Data need	Data query	Data source	Time frame	Frequency of data collection
Developing our library spaces in line with user needs	'How are students using the library space and how has this changed?'	Headcount User experience In-house loans	3 years 4 weeks 3 years	Daily, every 4 hours Daily, 9–5 Daily, morning
	'What do students want from their study spaces?'	User experience Surveys Common enquiries related to spaces	3 weeks 3 weeks 3 years	Daily, 9–5 Over 3 weeks
	'What are the top enquiries relating to library spaces?'	Space-related enquiries	3 years	All data compared

Plan your data collection

There are a lot of facets to be aware of when collecting data manually. However, regardless of the data collection method you are using, there are a few things to be aware of when deciding the details of your approach:

- *What resources are required?* Identifying what resources are required for your different data collection options will enable you to make an informed decision on the best approach for you and your service. Resources required could include staff time, systems or equipment needed, likely training needs, and anything else that may be required to ensure this data collection is possible.
- *How can you make the process work for your staff?* If data collection seems likely to take a long time or be convoluted, think about how it can be simplified. Manual data collection can often be confusing so make your process simple and easy to follow. Remember that human intervention brings human error, so build in as little opportunity for things to go wrong as possible. One of the areas this applies to most is your systems and the way you set them up.
- *How will you input this data and where will you store it?* Storing outside a computer is not an option, so this is a chance for you to be creative with your use of systems. While you will likely choose some form of spreadsheet to store raw data (e.g. Microsoft Excel or Google Sheets as an excellent free alternative) think about using or acquiring a system for inputting data too. The free or widely available options include

28   DATA-DRIVEN DECISIONS

Microsoft and Google Forms, which are great options in the first instance for building up your data-driven decisions culture and for less sophisticated data needs. Using Google Forms, you can collect data for certain fields, narrow it down to data type (e.g. numbers) and ensure that fields are completed, all of which contribute to minimising the chance for human error. For more complex data needs, for combining data collection and analysis, and for in-house analytics, you may want to consider purchasing data collection software such as LibInsight from Springshare LLC. We will talk more about setting up storage for your data sources later in this chapter.

Manual data collection

Manual data collection encompasses the collection and inputting of data by a member of staff, from counting the number of trolleys to be shelved, to inputting enquiries into a premade template. The essence of manual data collection is exactly what you'd expect – data which requires manual intervention in order to be collected and stored. Thus whatever data you collect manually has a direct cost in staff hours used. This can put many library managers off collecting data at all, as data collection seems less important than other staff tasks, and some staff give negative feedback about using their time for data collection. It is therefore more difficult to manage manual than automated data collection and important to get it right. No pressure!

Start collecting data

We are now ready to start collecting data. Look at Table A.1 and choose a data source that requires manual data collection. Using the points outlined in the bullet list above, fill in the manual data collection plan of Table A.2 with what your data collection process will be. Don't worry if your data collection methods may change some of the decisions you made when completing a time frame – this is okay! We should develop and change our choices when we receive new information.

> **Examples of manual data collection**
> Enquiry stats
> Time to shelve trolleys
> Use of non-catalogued items
> Time between return and to shelf

Table 4.4 opposite is an example of a completed manual data collection plan for a university library.

STEP 2: COLLECT   29

Table 4.4 *Manual data collection plan for a university library*

	Data source	Timeframe	Frequency
	Headcount data	3 years	4 times daily
Proposed collection method	Staff walk around the library and count how many people are in each space		
Specifics (where, what, how, what is included and excluded, etc.)	Staff count all users whether sitting or standing All parts of library (excluding the entrance) Do not count library staff		
How data is stored	Data is counted and broken down by area: • enquiry desk • ground floor silent zone • 1st floor silent zone • 1st floor collaboration space • meeting rooms broken down by individual room. Store on spreadsheet saved in shared drive, data folder		
How data is input	Staff use Microsoft form to input on iPad or mobile device		
Potential issues and risks	Staff forget to collect data Incorrect data is input		
Resources required	iPad Staff hours (approve 2 hours daily)		
Process what overlap or have potential to combine	Trolley logging Roving enquiry service		

Staff input and trials

Once you have decided on a potential method for your manual data collection, trial it with your staff (or if you are a solo professional try it out yourself). Something may seem like a perfect solution on paper but in practice or in the long term it simply may not be feasible. Trialling, gaining feedback and making amendments is vital to ensuring that you have a robust method of data collection in place.

Where possible, get a range of staff to trial your data collection method. Ensure that you trial this method across the different time periods you will be collecting. Consider making a standardised feedback form that your staff have access to before completing the trial, so they know key things to be aware of and to feedback on. These could explore things such as:

• ease of process
• barriers to completing process
• time of process (either from start to finish or broken into facets)

30 DATA-DRIVEN DECISIONS

- ease of input or feedback on equipment needs
- how to give general feedback.

Once you have collected your feedback, make any possible changes to your method and get a second round of feedback. Depending on the extent of your data collection you could do this multiple times before you land on a finalised data collection method.

Be aware of the difference between negative feedback given because a process needs to be improved, and poor feedback given because the person involved has negative perceptions or feelings towards data collection. Both are important to take heed of, but the latter is not a reason to stop data collection or overhaul a process which is necessary.

Set up data storage the right way

By now you should have an idea of your approach to manual data collection and your timeframes and at least have some initial thoughts about what tool you may use to input and store data. The next step (before beginning data collection) is to set up your data storage.

There are two broad ways of setting up initial storage of data:

- purchase a system which has a sophisticated interface for inputting data
- create your own system, likely using some kind of form and spreadsheet.

For now, we will focus on the latter.

Use spreadsheets

The way you choose to lay out and organise your data in a spreadsheet is one of the most impactful decisions to make in ensuring the effectiveness and long-term usability of your data. It may seem of minimal importance compared with say choosing the data to collect in the first place, but the way you organise data determines who can use it, how it's used, and how often it's used. Perhaps most importantly, though, correctly organising your data will save you and your colleagues a lot of time.

Organising data

There are three main aims we can aspire to when organising data: *the data is easy to find, easy to analyse, and easy to understand.*

STEP 2: COLLECT   31

The best way to show this is by thinking of a less than ideal example of how to organise data and its impact, as shown in Table 4.5. This spreadsheet is based on a real example that I came across which was used to manage headcount data.

Table 4.5   *Example of a poorly laid out spreadsheet*

	01:00				06:00				11:00			
	Lvl 1	Lvl 2	Lvl 3	Total	Lvl 1	Lvl 2	Lvl 3	Total	Lvl 1	Lvl 2	Lvl 3	Total
01/01/2020	0	2	1	3	5	3	7	15	45	30	12	87
02/01/2020	3	0	2	5	3	6	6	15	50	23	20	93
03/01/2020	5	7	2	14	2	7	3	12	30	37	14	81
04/01/2020	6	9	0	15	0	6	7	13	25	45	15	85
06/01/2020	3	0	2	5	3	6	6	15	50	23	20	93
07/01/2020	2	2	1	5	1	2	4	7	67	30	40	137
08/01/2020	4	1	0	5	1	0	0	1	53	32	22	107
09/01/2020	0	0	2	2	1	2	0	3	23	42	11	76
10/01/2020	1	0	1	2	4	0	1	5	11	15	22	48
11/01/2020	6	9	0	15	0	6	7	13	25	45	15	85
13/01/2020	3	0	2	5	3	6	6	15	50	23	20	93
14/01/2020	2	2	1	5	1	2	4	7	67	30	40	137

Let's think about what is wrong with the organisation of this spreadsheet in relation to our three aims:

- *Easy to find* There are a few key issues with this spreadsheet which makes the data hard to find. First, there are no headings or additional labels to make it clear what data is where. This might not seem so bad with this small snapshot, but in the real spreadsheet, the layout is so confusing that you would need to do a significant amount of work to find a particular date or time period. Further, the spreadsheet lacks additional information which might be needed for analysis, such as identifying the days of the week. Equally, the lack of summary or consistent totalling is another barrier to finding the right data. At present the way that the totals are used (at the end of each hour, with no grand totals) means that you would need to do some heavy editing if you wanted to use the data in any other way than how it is currently set out.
- *Easy to understand* Making the data clear and easy to understand is vital in ensuring that it can be used in future and by different people. In this spreadsheet the lack of headings and labels is a large barrier to understanding what the data is and the context or background of the data. No explanation is given for the abbreviation used. Key choices have been made which are confusing to users unless they made the spreadsheet, for example, the different coloured rows. My initial assumption was that the coloured rows refer to Saturday and Sundays when in fact they refer to Friday and Saturday. If you look closely, you

32   DATA-DRIVEN DECISIONS

will also notice that there are only six days logged each week. Without any additional information on this spreadsheet, that is very easy to miss and is likely to lead to mistakes being made when analysing and drawing conclusions from the data.

- *Easy to analyse* One of the worst things about this spreadsheet is how difficult it is to analyse it. We've already referenced the lack of highlights and regular totals. To make any analysis outside calculating the total hours we would need to do some significant work to highlight the relevant data because of the unhelpful layout. We also know that the lack of additional information would make breaking down data by day of the week or similar particularly difficult. This spreadsheet is the opposite of what we need to analyse and use data effectively.

Consider what you could you do differently:

- Think about how you organise dates and times on your spreadsheet: have you tried a few layouts to see what is easier to manage? Is there a way to break this information down, such as using colour to break it up (and noting this choice!).
- Include totals outside the core data (at the end or on a new sheet).
- Think about what totals will be helpful and put formulas in place when you first set up your spreadsheet.
- Ensure that your spreadsheet is set up with the correct data types and format for each column so that you can use formulas to speed up any analysis.
- Include additional information which will save time later (such as days of the week).
- Avoid freezing aspects of the data on your spreadsheet; instead freeze only heading columns.
- Make sure that your headings are meaningful.

Think about how you can make it as easy as possible to pull quick data and more detailed data from your spreadsheet. One of the real problems with the example given in Table 4.5 is how much individual copy and pasting would be needed to compare days or times, which not only wastes staff time but adds additional and unnecessary barriers to using data frequently, creates more opportunities for mistakes, and ends in duplicated effort.

To solve this, you can think about how you might be able to add in subtotals that could be useful (e.g. if you are collecting data multiple times during a day, perhaps add a daily total). You could also think about how the

STEP 2: COLLECT   33

data can be narrowed down to give the specific data needed, or to support analysis. The layout of your data here is important, but consider using labels. For example, you might have an additional column next to your dates with the days of the week, which could then easily be used for analytical purposes depending on the day of the week.

Another way to make your data more accessible and usable when organising a spreadsheet is to add a separate highlights sheet. If you do this in the first instance you can edit the layout of your data accordingly, and use formulas to update the highlights sheet automatically. This is another key reason for taking the time to organise data as using formulas only saves time if you don't need to intervene manually each time you need information.

Table 4.6 shows an example of the same data as that provided in Table 4.5 in a more manageable spreadsheet. We have removed the totals in the middle of the data and included additional labels.

Table 4.6   *Headcount of occupancy of library, 1–14 January 2020, by level and time; example of a well laid out spreadsheet*

			01:00			06:00			11:00		
Week number	Week day	Date	Lvl 1	Lvl 2	Lvl 3	Lvl 1	Lvl 2	Lvl 3	Lvl 1	Lvl 2	Lvl 3
Week 1	Wednesday	01/01/2020	0	2	1	5	3	7	45	30	12
Week 1	Thursday	02/01/2020	3	0	2	3	6	6	50	23	20
Week 1	Friday	03/01/2020	5	7	2	2	7	3	30	37	14
Week 1	Saturday	04/01/2020	6	9	0	0	6	7	25	45	15
Week 2	Monday	06/01/2020	3	0	2	3	6	6	50	23	20
Week 2	Tuesday	07/01/2020	2	2	1	1	2	4	67	30	40
Week 2	Wednesday	08/01/2020	4	1	0	1	0	0	53	32	22
Week 2	Thursday	09/01/2020	0	0	2	1	2	0	23	42	11
Week 2	Friday	10/01/2020	1	0	1	4	0	1	11	15	22
Week 2	Saturday	11/01/2020	6	9	0	0	6	7	25	45	15
Week 3	Monday	13/01/2020	3	0	2	3	6	6	50	23	20
Week 3	Tuesday	14/01/2020	2	2	1	1	2	4	67	30	40

Lvl = Level

Table 4.7 on the next page shows an additional sheet with daily totals. By including daily totals on a running formula it is easy to break down the data by different facets. You can also easily incorporate weekly, monthly and running totals either into a new sheet or attached to the daily totals.

Embed manual data collection into regular practice

The next step is to explore how you can embed manual data collection into regular practice. For shorter term data collection this may seem less important, but whatever period you collect data for, ensure that the data is actually being collected and its collection is embedded into regular practice.

34 DATA-DRIVEN DECISIONS

Table 4.7 *Headcount of occupancy of library, 1–14 January 2020, by level and time, with daily totals*

Week number	Week day	Date	Daily total	Daily Lvl 1 total	Daily Lvl 2 total	Daily Lvl 3 total	01:00 total	06:00 total	11:00 total
Week 1	Wednesday	01/01/2020	105	50	35	20	3	15	87
Week 1	Thursday	02/01/2020	113	56	29	28	5	15	93
Week 1	Friday	03/01/2020	107	37	51	19	14	12	81
Week 1	Saturday	04/01/2020	113	31	60	22	15	13	85
Week 2	Monday	06/01/2020	113	56	29	28	5	15	93
Week 2	Tuesday	07/01/2020	149	70	34	45	5	7	137
Week 2	Wednesday	08/01/2020	113	58	33	22	5	1	107
Week 2	Thursday	09/01/2020	81	24	44	13	2	3	76
Week 2	Friday	10/01/2020	55	16	15	24	2	5	48
Week 2	Saturday	11/01/2020	113	31	60	22	15	13	85
Week 3	Monday	13/01/2020	113	56	29	28	5	15	93
Week 3	Tuesday	14/01/2020	149	70	34	45	5	7	137

Lvl = Level

There are a few ways to embed manual data collection into regular practice:

- Combine your data collection timetable with your regular staff timetable.
- Involve staff in the planning processes, giving as much time as possible to remind staff that data collection is beginning.
- For longer data collection plans, take a few weeks as a soft launch so that any missed collection periods or issues can be addressed without impact on the data, so staff have time to acclimatise to the change.
- Appoint peer staff champions to support other staff through the change and remind them of the data collection without managerial intervention.
- Ensure that data collection is a standing item on any relevant meetings, and that staff have a chance to discuss how it is going and that you respond to issues as they arise.
- Be willing to adapt and change, particularly in the early stages.

Amy's top tips for manual data collection

Many steps are involved in planning how to collect data effectively, but it is difficult to give direct support without knowing how you will use the data you collect. Although I can't describe exactly how to plan each type of manual data collection, I have put together some top tips alongside the step-by-step process given above that you can use to decide what method to take and to develop your approach towards collecting data manually:

- *Combine manual data collection with other data collection methods already in place* As mentioned above, a seriously difficult aspect of managing manual data collection is the staff time that it requires. Therefore save time wherever possible by combining your data collection processes. This won't work for everything, but there may be instances where you can edit a separate process to fit it in with a new process, which will ultimately save you time on both. For example, if you are collecting two lots of data which require staff to move around the library building, these two pieces of data could be collected at the same time. The easiest way to do this is to map out the different data collection processes you have and identify similarities or possible similarities and work from there. It won't be possible for everything, but it will save you time to think about this early on and keep it under review.

- *Use direct input where possible* When planning your manual data collection process, think not just about how you are going to collect the data, but also where and how you are going to input and store that data. Directly input the data into the location where the data is stored, immediately after collecting it. *Do not keep data on pieces of paper and input it to a spreadsheet at a later date.* Manually inputting data from paper and onto a spreadsheet or programme requires a significant amount of staff time, means that the data has a time lag (potentially a large one) and offers more chance for errors in the recording of data. It also completely removes the rest of the process from data input which is a key aspect of the data collection, therefore removing opportunities for engagement. Do not do it. Even if you think it is a good solution to start with – don't do it. If you think it won't have that much impact – don't do it. I say it with love, I say it with force to save you and your future data lovers many headaches. Just don't do it, okay?

- *Save your data* It is upsettingly easy to lose data or create problems for your service in the future if you don't have good storage practices. Create clear locations for your data and save all appropriate data in the same place. If your organisation changes its systems, move your data. I cannot express how important it is that your data is all easily findable and together so that your hard work doesn't eventually go to waste by someone redoing it! Ensure your document titles are clear and descriptive. The aim in data-driven decision making is to create a lasting wealth of data to use in the future, and poorly named documents are one of the main barriers to this. Keep a directory document with file names, locations and explanations of what is in these files. Don't underestimate the importance of backing up your data and having a back-up schedule. This is particularly important when you are using different systems to log and store your data.

- *Plan for all staff abilities and mistakes* This has been mentioned already:

recognise that the nature of using online systems and working with people is that things will go wrong, so work this fact into your processes. For staff inputting, lock down as many of the fields as possible so that information has to be inputted in relevant fields and must be in the correct format. Never assume that staff have had enough training, always offer regular refresher training and keep an eye on what is inputted to address any issues as they arise.

Automated data collection

Let's start this section by acknowledging how much you have taken in for the first part of this chapter, and that you are doing a great job to have got to this point. Fortunately, in comparison with manual data collection, learning about automated data collection is going to feel like a breeze.

Automated data collection is data taken from sources where the data is being collected automatically, for example, usage data from a LMS or from gate count systems. It can be easy to assume that automated data collection means that you don't have to do anything . . . but this would be a pretty pointless section if that were the case!

If everything is already collected, what do you need to do with automated data?

Even though the data has already been collected and stored, the problem with automated data collection is that there is so much data from so much time, so do some work to decide and pull the relevant data, which naturally requires a bit of forward planning.

Timeframe

Just as with manual data collection, think about your timeframe. Unlike manual data collection, instead of thinking about the maximum amount of data and timeframes you need, when dealing with automated data, focus more on how you can narrow down your data. The difference between planning your timeframes for automated and manual data collection is really that you are working forward with manual and backwards with automated.

The first thing to focus on when deciding your timeframe for automated data is what period of data to examine. The benefit of automated data is that you have a wealth of data often spanning years that you can pull from, but just as with manual data collection you still need to narrow down to a relevant period. You could easily pick a single week or month to look at, but don't forget the importance of making relative comparisons and appropriate timeframes for decision making.

Once you have decided your time period, depending on your system you may need to narrow down further by days of week, times of day and so on. You don't need to be as conservative when collecting your data from automated sources as when collecting it manually as using more data does not take up more staff time. However, make sure you are analysing whatever data you choose in a sensitive and appropriate way for the data you have collected (see more about this in Chapter 6).

Sorting data

The last step to take when collecting automated data is to sort and manage it. We will discuss this step in more detail in our next chapter, but there are a few things to consider at this point.

Depending on the system from which you are downloading your data, it may be possible to choose the layout of the spreadsheet that is created from this data. If this is not the case, you will instead need to reorganise your spreadsheet according to the specific needs you have for your data once downloaded. As with manual data collection this process is really important for when you come to your mapping and analysing stage. While you don't need to have running tallies for ongoing usage of the data in the same way as you do with manual data collection, it is a good idea to still have a highlights sheet made, and to include any totals which you require to complete further analysis.

This is the point where the step-by-step process begins to blur a little bit. How do you base a plan for your data on what you want to analyse when you don't know about analysing yet? There is no simple way to separate some of these steps, so accept that you need to come back to this stage of your data collection once you have learned about mapping and analysis. Then with all the knowledge you will have gained by that point you can make changes to the way you have organised your data. Maybe pop a little sticky note or bookmark here as a reminder to yourself.

Saving data

Just as you did with your manual data collection, save any data you extract and work on from automated sources in an appropriate place. It is much easier with automated data to forget to save appropriately, and even easier still to assume that you can just pull the same data again and that it doesn't matter if you lose this particular spreadsheet. Do not fall into these traps!

Why? Well, while it's not wrong that you could pull the data you need again at a later date, when you start using data regularly, redownloading reports and organising data when you have already worked on it is a monumental waste of time.

Another very important reason to save your reports properly is so you can trace back to important data you will use for decision-making purposes. In creating a data-driven service you will find that data is required more and more, and different examples and visuals of the data will be required depending on who is using it. You may submit a lovely report with excellent graphs to a colleague, and they come back and ask for more detail, or a different view of the graph. Equally, as we are all human and all fallible, you may well create and use visualisations of your data which could be improved on or may even have mistakes. Being able to look back at your original data is vital.

When saving your data:

> If you have invested in software that stores and helps you analyse your data, you still need to complete the steps above, but instead make sure you are sorting your data based on the needs of the system and in line with your other data. Save your spreadsheet or CSV file in a safe space just in case anything goes wrong or anything happens with the data in your system.
>
> Ensure you include the system and upload date in your file name!

- Have a shared location in which you save the original unedited data or spreadsheets in one folder and the edited spreadsheets in another folder.
- Move any graphs you create into a separate sheet on your spreadsheet.

Summary

Getting your data collection right can seem like a daunting task, but the key thing to remember is that we're all learning all the time. If you reflect on your data collection methods and realise there are things you need to do differently, you are doing something right.

There are a lot of steps and tips in this chapter, but the key takeaway should be to plan, plan and plan some more. Don't forget to involve your colleagues too, then you will be off to a very good start.

5 Step 3: Map

Introduction

In this chapter we will look at mapping our data, what mapping our data means, and why we should care about it.

- what mapping is (page 39)
- how to make data comparable (page 40)
- key skills for mapping (page 48)
- how to create a map of data (page 52)

What is mapping?

You will be used to the way this works by now – we start with the big question of the chapter: what is data mapping?

Taking a very simple view, data mapping is the translating, overlaying and visualising of different sources of data to enable you to gain a more thorough understanding and to explore new and more complicated data needs which you identified in Step 1. It is the intermediate step between data collection and data analysis. While it is possible to jump directly from collection to analysis, you will miss out on a really vital part of moving towards data-driven decision making and creating a culture of it.

In this chapter we look at mapping for specific data.

Why is mapping important?

To truly move towards a culture of making data-driven decisions, you need to map your data. The heart of data-driven decision making is finding genuine understanding and truths from your data so you can make the best possible decisions for your service and your users. Mapping really is the best way to do this (outside collecting and using data in the first place!). By mapping your data, you will be able to find patterns and trends which often aren't visible when looking at only one source of data. When done well, mapping can open avenues leading to developments and decisions you may not have known were

> My husband had a lovely analogy while I was explaining this chapter to him: data collection is buying the car, mapping your data is knowing the route, and analysis is actually getting to your destination.

needed. It is a tough technique to learn and to get right, but the pay-off really is worth it.

Making data comparable (normalising)

There are a fair few steps to take before you can begin to draw up your data map. One of the most important is to make your data comparable, so let's start with that.

As mentioned in the chapter introduction, the idea with creating a map of your data is that you overlay different data sources and types to gain a more extensive and in-depth understanding of a situation. You can think of overlaying data like having multiple pieces of tracing paper with different parts of the same drawing on – let's use a drawing of a chicken as an example. The ideal situation is that you can lay these on top of one another and they all fit together nicely, are all the right size, and you can clearly see without a doubt that together the tracing paper makes said chicken. What if the tracing paper or parts of the picture are all different sizes, or there are gaps in some of the drawings, or you are missing a piece? You could put all of these together and you might think you actually have a drawing of a dinosaur. For the different pieces to work together to give the right picture they must be comparable. It's exactly the same with mapping and overlaying data. Make sure that the different pieces of data actually work together, or you could get the wrong picture! This process of making your data comparable is called normalising.

There are too many variations possible in your data for us to cover every way you can look at making it comparable. I've selected some of the key things to think about, but you will find more specific examples when creating your map.

Dates and times

Something that will certainly come up when you are mapping is the dates and times of your data. For both visualisations (later in this chapter) and analysis (next chapter), it is really important that you normalise dates and times.

For dates, make sure you are using data of the same period. You can't overlay data from one data source from 2019 and another data source from 2020, or one from January and another from March. For your map to be able to show trends they need to be from the same time. Note – this only refers to comparing different data sources (e.g. headcount data and enquiry data). You can compare data from the same data source of different time periods.

Also look at the period of collection and how this is displayed. If one piece of data is collected monthly and one piece of data daily, decide whether you want to combine your data and how. For overlaying data with different periods of collection you can make your data comparable in a couple of ways:

- Add up data taken more frequently until you have the upper period (e.g. add your daily totals to make a monthly total instead).
- Average your upper period into your lower period of data collection (e.g. divide your monthly total to get an average weekly or daily total).

While you can overlay data with different periods of collection you want them to be as close as possible to ensure that you can later complete a more accurate analysis, and that your visualisations actually work.

Let's look at a few graphs to see how this can make a difference. In the library used for these examples, book loans are collected automatically on the LMS and gate counts are logged as a total on the first of each month.

Figure 5.1 on the next page shows the visualisation we create without normalising the data, and is less than helpful. We cannot make any comparisons or analysis from this. Even with a shorter snippet of time we would still end with the visualisation shown in Figure 5.2, which again doesn't help us gain any wider understanding.

However, if we normalise the data to make it more comparable we can draw real conclusions.

In Figure 5.3 we have an example of an upper normalisation (normalising to the month) and can start to identify trends across both sets of data and actually understand it.

42 DATA-DRIVEN DECISIONS

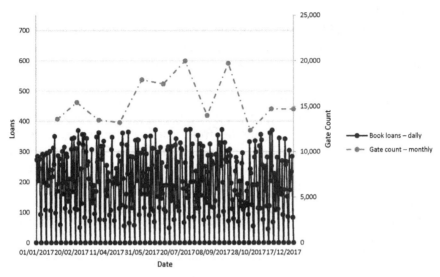

Figure 5.1 *Daily book loans and monthly gate count, May 2017; an example of poorly mapped data which hasn't been normalised*

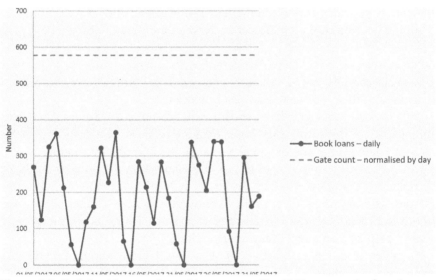

Figure 5.2 *Daily book loans and monthly gate count, May 2017; an example of poorly mapped data which has been normalised*

We can also normalise the lower set of data (normalising by day) as shown in Figure 5.4.

This is a much less useful visualisation than Figure 5.3. When normalising the lower set of data you can often end up with less helpful data, particularly

STEP 3: MAP   43

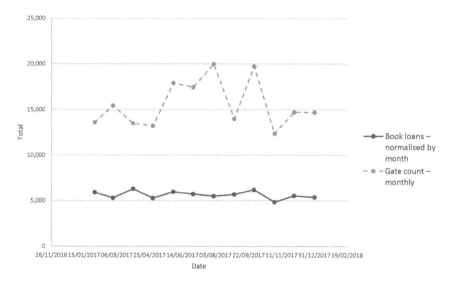

Figure 5.3 *Monthly loans and gate count, 2017; an example of normalised and mapped data*

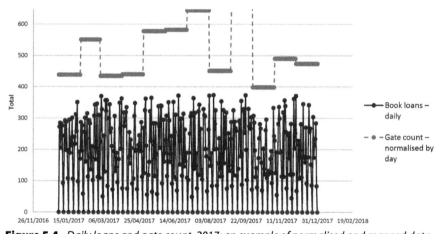

Figure 5.4 *Daily loans and gate count, 2017; an example of normalised and mapped data*

when the difference in period is large (e.g. day to month as in Figure 5.4). You need to choose what gives you the most useful information and best represents your service.

It can be difficult to know where to start with normalising, even when thinking of a specific area such as dates and times. To help you get there, here are some examples of when and how you need to normalise data specifically regarding dates and times.

44   DATA-DRIVEN DECISIONS

Also, just a note on the data in these figures. It's entirely fabricated, so don't try and read too much into anything you see in them!

> Remember that the point of mapping is to be able to make accurate decisions based on your data, which is why we are normalising it. We don't ever want to present falsified data, so be transparent about the work you have done and most importantly why.

Weekday or weekend?

Paying attention to whether your data has been collected on a weekend or weekday is one of the simplest things to tackle when making your data comparable. If you have a service which operates at weekends and some data (e.g. loan statistics) is collected on weekend days, take this into account when creating your data map to gain an accurate understanding of your loan statistics. If you map one piece of data which includes weekends and one which doesn't, remove the weekend data completely from your daily, weekly or monthly totals for this particular map. An alternative would be to make it

> In any analysis, fully document and reference any changes you make to your data for the purpose of normalising it. There is more on this in Chapter 6, meanwhile think about how and where you are going to store data.

extremely clear that this data is missing, for example, by including weekly statistics which include weekend days and putting a note on the Saturday and Sunday stating that X data is not available.

What you absolutely shouldn't do is average or condense the seven days of data into five days to match the other data for your map. Why? *Because it will give an inaccurate picture and comparison*! Remember the dinosaur folks.

Hours in a working day

On a similar vein, you also need to account for hours in a working day. You may have certain days in the week where certain services are open for fewer hours than others, which naturally affects the amount of data that can be collected. Once again, normalise this data before mapping it. How you approach this will depend on the specific needs of your service. There may be some areas where having data from different hours in the day wouldn't have a negative impact on the overall picture from a mapping point of view, but be absolutely certain this is the case before deciding to use 'non-normalised' data on a map.

If you need to normalise your data for different hours, display the data by equivalent percentages. Alternatively, multiply the data on the shorter days to depict the likely data for this day as if it had the same working hours as another. As you don't want to present data which isn't real, include visualisations of the normalised and non-normalised examples together and make sure you have labelled them accurately.

Time-logged vs non-time-logged data

Time-logged data has been timestamped or collected across the day at dedicated times; non-time-logged data is data that you may only have totals for (e.g. daily, weekly). As a general rule with normalising two differing pieces of time-logged data normalise to the highest instance up to a day, so if one piece of data were collected three times in a day, and one 12, you would combine and average the data collected 12 times a day into the three 'slots' of the other piece of data.

When normalising time-logged against non-time-logged data at the top level of your map, total the timed data to make the two pieces of data comparable. Your hard work in collecting timed data has not been wasted, but for the purpose of a bigger picture exploration gained from this mapping you are focusing on a less granular view of the data.

Staffing

Data on staffing is one of the most important things to normalise and can and should be used when making decisions that affect staff and staffing, whether on deployment of resources, staffing levels, the capacity for undertaking new projects or anything else. If you are making decisions for staff always back them up with your knowledge, feedback from staff *and* data. When used correctly data can help us to gain a truer understanding of a situation outside our own biases and preconceptions, which often influences staffing choices.

When normalising staffing data always consider the full-time equivalent (FTE) of individual staff, teams and hours of shifts.

Working out FTEs

When calculating staffing levels it is essential to consider staff hours to understand and map the situation accurately. It can be easy to compare teams or staff members within a team directly, for example, but if you haven't included the FTE in your mapping or analysis you can quickly draw incorrect conclusions.

Say you are an academic librarian looking at the number of teaching sessions delivered by each staff member within a single team. You might directly map

46   DATA-DRIVEN DECISIONS

this information against student loans and student numbers by subject to identify correlations in engagement. You could look at these two pieces of data and see that they match up well and don't need any normalising. The issue here will not show up at the mapping stage, but at the analysis stage. If you have any differences in FTE or part-time staff who are supporting subjects, then any understanding you gain will be skewed in this scenario. Therefore, work out the FTE and take this into account in your mapping.

You can use the formula below:

$$= \text{Number or data/FTE}$$

or

(the same equation but following mathematical convention)
$$= \text{number or data} *(1/\text{FTE})$$

If you are comparing say staff member X, who is a full-time member of staff and completed 10 sessions, with staff member Y who is 0.8 FTE and completed 7 sessions. You are trying to find out what 7 would be equivalent to if the two staff members were on the same hours – how many sessions would staff member Y complete if they worked full-time. Thus the number or data would be 7 (for the number of sessions) and the FTE would be 0.8:

$$7*(1/0.8) \text{ OR } 7/0.8 = 8.75$$

From this we can see that staff member Y is doing slightly fewer sessions than their full-time equivalent, but not necessarily so few that it would be a concern.

Translating data

Translating is one of the more involved processes in normalising data for mapping. To explain translating data, we need to go back to the different types of data we explored in Chapter 3. Our main reason for translating data is so that we can compare different types of data. We are going to stick to the simplified view of data types we took in Chapter 3 and focus on qualitative and quantitative data.

The big problem for mapping different types of data is qualitative data. Raw quantitative data is quick to sort and analyse, it's already in numbers, you can add it up easily; it's just great. Raw qualitative data on the other hand is a monster of free text and defies automation and quick analysis. It has its qualities, and it's very important when making data-driven decisions, but purely from a mapping and analysis standpoint? Well, let's move on.

When translating qualitative data you are doing exactly what you'd expect – translating raw data into numerical, quantifiable data. It can be time consuming, but the data you collect from qualitative data collection really can't be replicated in traditional quantitative data collection methods, so it is definitely worth the time.

Key steps for translating qualitative data
Coding
Coding is the most important step in translating your data. By coding our qualitative data, we give a structure to the data to understand and analyse the content. As you know, with qualitative data we often have free text input, or visual data (e.g. maps or drawings of the library space), neither of which can be input into a spreadsheet and compared against something like headcount data. Coding allows us to do this.

Coding is when you take a full overview of your raw qualitative data and create codes to group it. This is an iterative process, so you may find that you code a few times as you become more familiar with the data and find different anomalies. For much qualitative data, coding involves going through your data and identifying themes within it. You may do this by identifying common words and images as you go through your data, and then find synonyms of them or alternative images. If you have maps, split the map up into different sections and name them.

You will find outliers, and for the initial translation it's important to keep them in and create a separate theme (word) for them. This step can be done manually, or you can use a system.

Your final code should be a list of themes (words) which you can then use to sort your data. For example, if your data is a map showing where users are moving around the space you might have locations as your themes. If your data is user feedback the themes would come from the types of words and phrases coming up. You can learn more about this step in chapters 6 and 11.

Sorting
Once you have created your code you need to come up with a system to identify how your raw data is connected to your themes (how to sort your data).

A good way to do this is to use colour coding, however you may choose to number your data, or even print and cut your data and sort it into columns.

48   DATA-DRIVEN DECISIONS

Find the method that works for you, as long as you are clear about where each individual piece of data sits.

Once you have your method and are happy with it, sort your raw data into each theme. It may be that for free text and image data one piece of data falls into multiple themes – this is okay and should be noted. At this stage we want to capture as much as possible.

Sometimes you may have multiple layers of data to sort and translate. This is not a problem, but make sure you are sorting them appropriately by keeping relevant data with each other so it can be analysed in context later on.

Tidying

Finally, tidy up your translated data. When coding and sorting data, it is easy to miss close similarities in data and to create a more complicated translation than needed. This is really just an opportunity for you to step back for a day or two and return with fresh eyes. Look at the layout of your new raw translated data and use the skills you learned from Chapter 4 to tidy your spreadsheet and consider how else it might need to be organised.

After you have completed this work you will end up with a list of themes, and then the number of times each theme came up. Table 5.1 shows an example.

Table 5.1 *Example of qualitative data translated into themes: the subjects of feedback postcards in September*

Themes	Instances
Laptop loans	21
Temperature	19
Opening hours	12
Stock availability	24
Programme suggestions	8
Noise	4

Visualisation

Before we dive into the actual process of mapping we're going to run through some of the key skills you need to create your map.

Visualisations and displaying data

Data visualisation is a term that's thrown around by avid data users and can sound a bit intimidating, but it is just creating an image or picture of your data so you can see it better (graphs, we're talking about graphs). Good data visualisation allows us to gain a strong understanding of data quickly and is the first step to analysis.

> For this section you need to be comfortable with creating graphs in a spreadsheet or another piece of software (Power BI, etc.). If you are not, find out how to create graphs and use pivot tables. Look at what software your institution has available already and read about it as it may be a real help to you!

A wealth of systems and software have been created specifically to make data visualisations easier, and if you have the resources I encourage you to check them out. However, you need a good understanding of what makes a good visualisation to use them.

In theory creating a graph on a spreadsheet isn't too difficult – just a few steps and you are done – but it is more tricky to make sure that the graph truly represents the data. Now, I can imagine some confused faces here – if the graph is made from the data how can it not be a true representation? Well, depending on the choices you make in your visualisation, you can easily misrepresent that data, which can in turn lead to incorrect analysis. Don't forget, it is your responsibility as a handler of data to present and interpret it correctly. Misrepresenting data can lead to poor decisions being made, and most importantly conveys falsehoods.

Figure 5.5 on the following page shows an example of how we can easily misrepresent data. It shows the cumulative total of loans made over each day of a week, however the way the data is presented makes it look as if we have the most loans on Friday, when actually we have the same number of loans each day. Thinking about how your data is going to be understood is pivotal to creating clear visualisations and good data practices.

Visualisation commandments

These are the visualisation commandments:

- *Always use the right kind of graph for your data* Choose the graph that best shows the full extent of the data you are trying to understand; for example, pie charts can be excellent for understanding a breakdown of enquiry types, or split of user types and library usage, but are not appropriate for displaying dates.
- *Always label your graphs appropriately* Give them precise captions including dates where relevant, look at how your axis is labelled, how your different pieces of data are labelled, if that information is readable

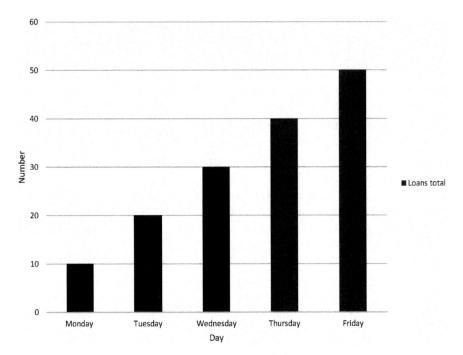

Figure 5.5 *Loans by day of week; an example of misleading data*

and that different parts of the graph are clear. Explain abbreviations and different types of notation, if used.

- *Always look at how your data is presented* If you are overlaying and comparing two data sources in one graph (which you will be for mapping) make sure that the graph is presented in a readable way and that the data is still understandable; if you have one set of data in the thousands and another on the same graph in the tens you may need to have a second axis, and perhaps a combination of line and bar to better represent the data.
- *Always try a few visualisations before deciding* Try laying out your data in a different way so you can be sure that the visualisation you choose is the right one and that you don't end up just using the visualisations you are used to.
- *Always use appropriate colours and patterns* Make sure that your colours are easy to see and differentiate; bold colours are best as a general rule, and stark differences in shade of the same colour family for lots of data. Include patterns or shading (dashed or dotted lines or filled columns) on your data to make sure it is clear and accessible to everyone.

Finally, consider how many sources of data you can fit into one graph. There is a balance to strike – it depends on what the data is that you are wanting to overlay and visualise. As a general rule, the key thing to look out for is how readable the graph is. If you get to the point that you have no idea what the data means any more when looking at your graph, you have probably put too much in.

For example, Figure 5.6 shows a graph of headcount data for each area and loans by specified hour.

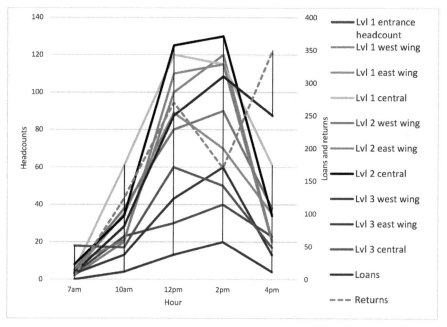

Lvl = Level

Figure 5.6 *Average headcount by area and hourly loans; an example of poorly mapped data from multiple data sources*

There is so much data in Figure 5.6 that it is almost impossible to get any information from it. Even though there are only three data sources (headcount, loan and return data), it's really tough to understand. There is so much data that you cannot make connections between the colour on the graph and data, cannot map trends very easily, and cannot differentiate between the types of data on the graph. Ideally you would present much less data in this figure, using a combination of line and column, and even perhaps multiple graphs to show snippets of the data and analyse it from there.

52   DATA-DRIVEN DECISIONS

In comparison, Figure 5.7 shows another graph with three data sources, but a more effective approach to visualisation.

In Figure 5.7 it is obvious that the comparison is between loans, book orders and current items in the repository, and we can see clear trends. Equally the patterns are clearer and the data works effectively with each other.

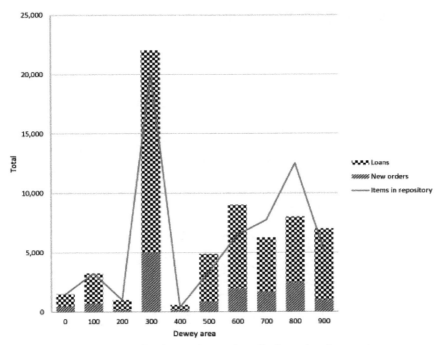

Figure 5.7   *Loans compared with items in repository (by Dewey) and new orders; an example of mapped data from three data sources*

Creating a map of your data

Now you have all the possible skills and background you need we can explore creating a map of your data. A reminder on our definition of mapping: it is the translating, overlaying and visualising of *multiple sources* of data to gain a truer understanding of how the data compares with each other.

There are two approaches to mapping – mapping for a specific data need (essentially mapping on a smaller scale) and mapping for entire service understanding. Mapping for entire service understanding and on a larger scale helps us identify information we didn't know we needed, opening up new avenues and approaches.

To create a map of your data:

STEP 3: MAP   53

- *Identify what data you will map* Find the different data sources that will answer any specific data need.
- *Translate and normalise your data.*
- *Overlay your data* Get your data either in a spreadsheet or your visualisation tool in a way that can be turned into a graph.
- *Create your visualisation* For a single data need ideally each data source will be visible in a single visualisation. You can then show different breakdowns and facets of all this data in different graphs, for example, you may have a totals graph, a graph broken down by week and so on.

> You may already have a system which allows you to store and design your map of visualisations. If not, consider using a website format, like Google Sites. Using a website is helpful as it allows you to use application programming interfaces to feed live data into it so your map updates along with new data.

- *Create a location for your visualisations and design a map* Creating and designing a home for your visualisations pulls the data together and gives you a map. This is not simply putting all of your graphs into a spreadsheet and being done with it. It is designing how your visualisations sit next to one another, how they relate, and adding in additional context and information.

Curating the layout for your map is once again a subjective process, so there's no right or wrong way to do it but there are a few things to think about:

- Think about how the map will be read. It often helps to start with your totals and broadest visualisations and work your way up to more detailed data. You can group different visualisations together as appropriate.
- Think about the size of your visualisations. Highlight key parts of your visualisations and take the reader through a journey in the map; increasing the size of certain graphs can achieve this.
- Add in context and additional information next to your visualisations.
- Don't forget to include a description of your map and data.

Figure 5.8 on the next page shows a bird's eye view example of a map for a specific data need.

The difference between creating a map for a specific data need and for your whole service comes down to how much data you include in your map. By using a site or tool such as Power BI (which is encouraged) you can break down a map into different pages, looking at different areas of data, or different levels of granularity.

54 DATA-DRIVEN DECISIONS

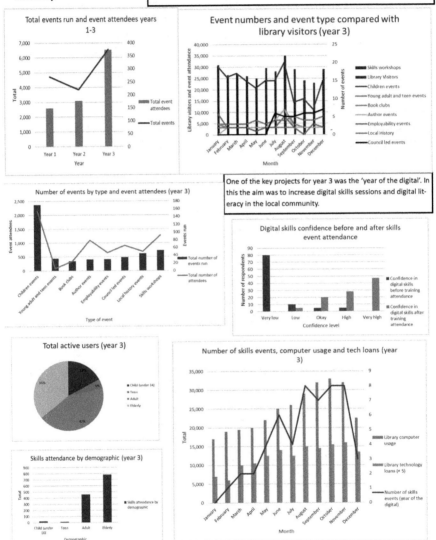

Figure 5.8 *Data map showing how the number of activities changed in a public library when a new events post was created*

STEP 3: MAP   55

Updating your map

The final consideration when creating a map of data is how to update your map. The long-term goal is to have a map that automatically updates from relevant systems and spreadsheets using application programming interfaces and system integrations. Naturally creating such a map involves a different set of skills and being able to use maps of data depends on many variables for your institution; it is certainly worth exploring them and seeing to what extent you can harness them.

If you cannot dive right into using APIs or system integrations, you will instead need to come up with a cycle for updating your map. This needs to be achievable but also frequent enough that the map can still be used daily to make decisions with confidence. As well as your cycle for updating you need to plan your process for updating and backing up your data (which is very similar to the approaches taken in Chapter 4).

Summary

Mapping data is a fundamental step to moving towards being able to make day-to-day data-driven decisions for your service. It allows you to make your data much more accessible and is a key tool in allowing it to be used to support wide-ranging decision making within your organisation.

Mapping your data is really a creative step, with fewer boundaries and parameters than a lot of the tasks involved in data-driven decision making, so it might seem overwhelming or less defined. With practice and (as always) input from your colleagues this will become second nature in no time.

6 Step 4: Analyse

Introduction

Leading nicely on from the significant amount of groundwork you did in the mapping chapter, this chapter we're getting to the big stuff – analysing and drawing conclusions from your data. By the end of the chapter you will be comfortable and confident in making accurate and well-drawn conclusions from single sets of data and mapped data. The key areas we will explore are:

- what analysis is (page 57)
- how to analyse data (page 58)
- how to draw conclusions from data (page 62).

What is analysis?

The most important thing to cover first when looking at analysis is the difference between your analysis and your conclusion. They are extremely closely linked, and it's easy to confuse the two. You can think of your analysis and conclusion as the start and end of the same journey. Analysis is the act of processing your data, and of highlighting and pulling out the relevant data for conclusion, and your conclusion is where you use all of this to actually identify what it means.

Massaging your data

Massaging data can cover a whole host of tasks and changes to the data you may need to complete to be able to draw conclusions. We take any raw data and look at totalling, averaging and any other steps that enable us to draw conclusions. There are lots of facets to this process but, luckily, we've actually

58 DATA-DRIVEN DECISIONS

already undertaken some initial massaging on our data in previous chapters. Let's quickly recap what we've already covered:

- laying out data and putting in place totals and subtotals
- translating and normalising to make data comparable
- all of the groundwork needed to create visualisations for your map.

The massaging that we've already covered was in the context of setting up data collection and mapping data, so there will be other instances where you need to do this same work, for example, for automated data, analysing single data sets or using the same data in multiple analyses.

Averaging

One of the aspects of data massaging which we haven't covered yet is averaging. We won't be going into all the ins and outs of averaging. We're instead going to stick to the basics, which you will use most of the time when analysing data.

You may remember at school being taught the three main types of averaging: mode, median and mean. This is one of the excellent times where a seemingly niche aspect of secondary education is actually going to come into use in adult life! The most useful type of averaging for us (and arguably the easiest to use) is mean averaging, so we will focus on that.

The mean average is where you take the total of your data (by adding up all of the values of your data) and divide that total by the total number of instances.

In Table 6.1 we add up all the total enquiries and divide that number (138) by the total number of instances, which in this case is 5. The average therefore is 28 (rounded up from 27.6).

Table 6.1 *Example figures for calculating a mean average*

Date	Total enquiries
01/01/2020	24
02/01/2020	36
03/01/2020	28
04/01/2020	29
05/01/2020	21

The mean average is particularly useful when making data-driven decisions as it takes all data into account and (when used correctly) gives the most accurate 'central tendency', which means we can gain the truest understanding of different periods or aspects of our data.

Making your averaging meaningful

One of the problems with using mean averaging is that it can be easily affected by significant peaks or drops and becomes less reliable the more of these peaks and drops you include in one average. Therefore averaging in context is key to making sure your averaged figure accurately depicts your data.

Averaging in context means making sure that when you choose what data to average you consider the context of that data. For example, let's imagine we're interested in getting a weekly average of the number of enquiries received over a period of a year. We could add up the values for the entire year and take our average from that, but it would likely give us an unhelpful or a heavily skewed average. This is because any big drops in data, for example, relating to weekends or (if you are in an academic or school library) out of term time, would be included and bring down your weekly average, making it seem that our quietest periods are much busier than normal and our busiest times are much quieter.

Instead choose periods of data where averaging would give you an accurate depiction of the general picture (sounds familiar, right?). If you work in an academic or school library you may want to average term time data separately from non-term time data. Equally, if you know your footfall at weekends is significantly lower or higher in usage than during the week you may choose to take averages for the week and weekend separately. When you are thinking about these things and your context you may realise that actually a weekly average is not what you need at all; perhaps it's averages by days of the week. Step back and think carefully about why you need an average of your data and what it's for before running head first into averaging indiscriminately.

Anomalies

As well as massaging the data and all the processes involved in getting data ready for analysis you also need to look at your data, identify any anomalies and attempt to understand them.

Anomalies are one-off and extreme peaks or troughs in your data which don't follow the regular pattern of the rest of it. Essentially, it is data which clearly deviates from the standard set by the rest of the data. It's important to take the time to identify anomalies as they can have big impacts on tools that

60 DATA-DRIVEN DECISIONS

enable you to analyse your data and draw conclusions, for example, about averaging and visualisations.

The easiest way to identify an anomaly will depend on how much data you have and what type it is. To identify any anomalies look at graphs of your data and your raw data, trying to identify anything which seems out of the ordinary. Naturally, we won't find all anomalies this way (which is a fairly manual process); another approach you could take is to filter and search for the lowest and highest figures in your data and take a close look at them. You can also identify anomalies during other stages of your data collection and analysis such as while creating averages and totals. Understanding your data and service will help you to notice anomalies at all stages (more on that in a moment).

Once you have identified your anomalies your next step is to identify why the anomalies are there or what created them. Often, there are errors in the data which need to be addressed, for example, incorrectly inputted or missing data. If you notice mistakes in your data, input an approximate figure for what the data likely would have been on that day by taking an average of similar periods of the same data. When you do this make sure you never delete any data. If you are fixing anomalies save the original data somewhere safe to be referred back to. Equally, make clear notes and highlight wherever you have made changes. Avoid falsifying data by documenting any changes you make to it to make it easier to understand or analyse, to ensure you can remember what you have done and allow others to understand the history of the data.

If your anomaly isn't a mistake, identify what other factors have led to this spike or drop in the data. You might want to compare the date with your calendar to see if there were any events or incidents that would have contributed to the anomaly. You can then decide what you will actually do about it on the basis of your understanding of the anomaly. You have a choice – when analysing your data do you want your anomaly taken into consideration or not? Once again, be really careful as you absolutely cannot falsify your data, so document any changes you make carefully: they should only be made with very good reason. Just as when correcting errors, if you choose to make changes find a reasonable figure based on averages of similar periods for the data.

Understand context

Although we have already discussed understanding the context of your data throughout this book, in every chapter, multiple times, there is indeed still more to think about. Needless to say it's an important aspect of all stages of a data-driven decision making process.

Understanding the context of your data allows you to manipulate and massage it properly, make better decisions about how to visualise it, and most importantly lets you draw the most accurate conclusions from it.

You need to:

- understand and know the additional information or factors that have an impact on your data at an individual level
- understand the wider context of your organisation, users and anything else which ultimately impacts how your service or library is used and why it is the way it is.

While you may have a perfect and infallible memory, I certainly do not, and it's likely that many of your colleagues are in the same boat as me. Good documentation is key to ensuring that you and any colleagues using your data (present and in future) can truly understand the context of your data and make use of this understanding.

Think about setting up a document which includes key pieces of information regarding your different data and its wider context for your organisation, which can be updated as appropriate. This document might include information on gaps in the data, when data may have changed (e.g. if there were changes to how data is collected, the amount collected), key events or information relating to certain periods, or anything else you can think of which is relevant for you and future data users to know. Sort this document and store information on the basis of the data collected and then the relevant information for each of these pieces of data. Consider including notes directly in your data with information about specific data instances and what has affected them (such as data not inputted or specific events).

Some of the widest contexts that affect your organisation can seem less important to document or to take into consideration, but they still have an impact, which needs to be considered for a much longer period of time. Let's take the 2020 pandemic, for example: everyone is affected and therefore aware of it so it would be impossible not to take the pandemic into account when analysing data from 2020. However, what about in three years' time when we compare the last five years of data to look at usage trends? The year 2020 itself is anomalous, and without identifying the impact that this year has had on usage (and likely the fallout of this on coming years) and understanding it we might make incorrect assumptions from the data. That's an extreme example, and likely the pandemic will never be overlooked within our data,

DATA-DRIVEN DECISIONS

but other significant changes like library moves or renovations, new services or dramatic service changes could easily be overlooked. Make sure these things are taken into consideration and documented within the context of the data too. If not for you, then for colleagues in the future who might look at this data.

Represent data correctly

It is important to represent data correctly. This is just about making sure you are not drawing conclusions that do not match what the data is showing you, and that you don't take the data out of context to support conclusions you want to make. All of the steps you have taken in your data-driven decision making journey until now have prepared you to ensure you are representing your data correctly.

> In using data to present your ideas or a situation, back-up your conclusions, and make decisions, you must ensure that the data you use is to the best of your knowledge a true representation of both the wider data and the real situation. You should never take data out of context to fit to or back up certain ideas.

Representing your data correctly is a simple process, just make sure you:

- *don't* draw conclusions for the wider service or situation based on a short period of data
- *don't* take a period of data which better represents your service or agrees with your ideas and present that over the larger more accurate period of data (unless only examining this single period)
- *don't* purposefully remove data which doesn't agree with what you want the data to present
- *don't* show single sets of data when the meaning changes with more information or context.

It's simple really: *do not misrepresent data.*

Conclusions

We have covered what data you need, how to collect it, how to map it, and all the different aspects of preparing your data for analysis and understanding your data. It's finally time to move on to the main event – how do you draw conclusions from your data? This is the final step in all of the pieces of understanding you have worked towards until now. By drawing conclusions, you are not just looking at and knowing what the data means at an individual level, you are making a wider statement of what the data means as a whole.

To start we focus on drawing conclusions specifically related to your data need. We will get to exploratory conclusions later on, but it's important we start with the basics. Let's cast our minds back to Chapter 3 where we first drew out our data needs and identified the data we would be collecting to answer that data need. You will know your data need well and have thought about it a lot in all the activities leading up to this point. Nonetheless, take some time here to once again review your data need, think about all of the context and knowledge you have for your organisation and data, and remind yourself why you actually have the data you have.

There's only one rule for drawing proper conclusions: *don't prejudge the data*.

The problem with collecting and analysing data and being human is that naturally we will have thoughts on what the data will tell us before we draw our official conclusions: we will even have an idea of what we want our data to tell us. This is normal, and there's no way to stop this happening to some extent. However, when you get to the stage of officially drawing your conclusions leave these prejudgements, hopes and preconceptions at the door.

When drawing conclusions, let the data and context drive your understanding. There's a reason we've done so much work until now to gain as full an understanding of the data as possible; let's not throw it away by diving into our conclusions with a clouded data eye.

Patterns, trends and surprises

The act of drawing conclusions from data is mostly about taking the time to step back and look at the relevant data with an almost bird's eye view.

Naturally the first thing to do is gather your visualised and massaged data. You should already have all of this together following the mapping that we explored in the last chapter, perhaps with some updates following checking for anomalies or adding additional averages. If you have done your mapping correctly you will have multiple visualisations and levels of data, depending on what data will answer your data need. You may also have multiple sources of data in your map as required by your data need. Next review and remind yourself of the contexts that have affected this data (again this should be included in your map). With all your data and information gathered together, you can start casting a critical eye over it.

Taking your bird's eye view of your map, start looking for any patterns visible, any trends and any surprises. Don't forget to note where your anomalies are and take those into account when identifying your patterns and trends. You don't base long-term or service-wide conclusions on anomalies but on regular patterns and outside trends.

You can, however, still use anomalies to reach some conclusions. For example, if you have a massive drop in loans and attendance because of an event in your institution, look at whether this might happen again and possibly take time to do something you haven't been able to do, like a big stock project, or planned maintenance. While you wouldn't draw a service-wide conclusion, you can still reach potentially useful conclusions and propose actions based on them.

Patterns

When looking for patterns try to see where your data is showing consistently similar patterns in your visualisation. For example, if you are looking at data across weekdays, you might see that the shape of the data is the same across all weeks, or that the pattern is the same for weeks during certain periods and there is a different pattern in others.

Draw out what patterns you can see, then you can base conclusions on those that are strong and consistent, as you can confidently know the situation that the data is presenting.

For example, Figure 6.1 shows a very consistent and strong pattern occurring year on year. We can use this data to draw the conclusion that activities from June to September will be significantly lower than for other months in the next year and make decisions accordingly.

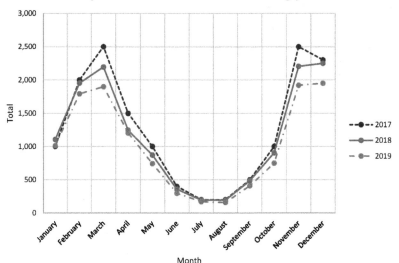

Figure 6.1 *Unnamed trends over three years*

Be aware of where there are no obvious patterns and then be much more careful about any conclusions you reach. Indeed you may find that you can't make accurate conclusions when there are no obvious patterns and want to understand why that is, which could open up a new data need. This will eventually lead you to find patterns that help you understand why you had no patterns in the first place.

Trends

A trend is the general direction in which something is developing or changing (OED Online, 2021b). To find trends take a similar approach as when looking for patterns. Once again step back and use a bird's eye view, but instead of looking for clear patterns, which show continuous expectations from the data, look for constant trends that show where the data is likely heading. In looking for trends, you are looking for a continuous move in data one way or another, or indeed at whether data has stayed the same over a period of time. For example, you may see that use of e-resources has consistently increased over a few years, or that a certain enquiry type has increased or declined.

For example, Figure 6.2 shows a strong increase in live chat enquiries, with the increase beginning to slow year on year, suggesting we may continue to see a small rise each year, but perhaps not to the same level that happened between years 2 and 3.

As with identifying patterns, be aware where trends are not clear. Do not draw broad conclusions based on data without clear trends, but you may find

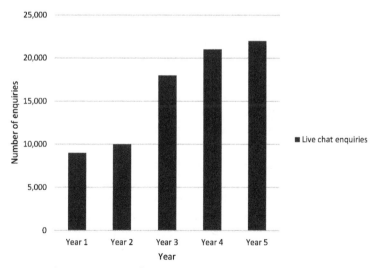

Figure 6.2 *Live chat enquiries over five years*

66 DATA-DRIVEN DECISIONS

that in examining the lack of trends alongside context, you can gain wider understanding and draw conclusions about why there are none.

Surprises

While looking at your patterns and trends, a big part of drawing conclusions is to identify any surprises based on your wider understanding of the data, and the context. Keep a note of what is as expected and what doesn't align with it to help you make decisions and draw true conclusions.

Drawing your conclusions

A conclusion is 'a judgement or statement arrived at by any reasoning process' (OED Online, 2021a). To draw conclusions bring all the information you have gathered throughout the process to make a final judgement on what the data is telling you. There is no set or simple way to do this, but it gets easier with time. Put very simply, to draw a conclusion look at the information gained while looking at your trends, patterns and surprises alongside your contextual information and make a final statement of understanding based on the data.

Example

Data need: reduce shelving and waiting for shelving time

Data source: shelving time by collection

Context: a library split into two collections: a high use collection in static shelving and a general collection in rolling stacks; the high use collection is made up of essential and further reading (from reading lists) and the general collection is all other items; books are periodically moved from the general collection and into the high use collection as they are added to reading lists; it has been noted that books are taking longer to be available on the shelves and that more trolleys are left waiting than at the start of the year

Visualisation of data: Figure 6.3 opposite shows a graph of the data collected to answer the data need

Conclusions: With the context and data shown in Figure 6.3 there is a clear trend showing that shelving in the high use collection has significantly increased over the year, while the shelving in the general collection has slightly decreased. Using this data we can pinpoint the issue to the high use collection and do some fact finding. Knowing that items are moved

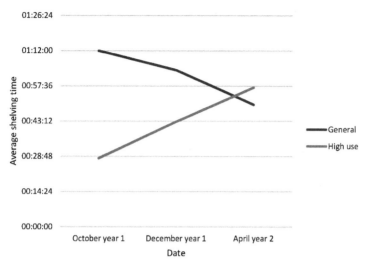

Figure 6.3 *Average shelving time for one trolley (October Year 1 to April Year 2); an example of normalised and mapped data*

regularly from the general collection into the high use collection, we could assume that part of the issue is shelves becoming fuller and therefore shelving taking longer as space is created. This was confirmed by comparing the number of items in the collection (which increased by 30% over six months) and a walk around the collection.

We can conclude that the reason for the increased time for shelving and between items being returned and available on the shelf is the overcrowding of the high use collection. This conclusion has enabled us to identify the need for a project to reduce the stock in the high use collection and to create new approaches to mapping the physical stock and space needs.

Check conclusions

When you have drawn your conclusions take some time to sanity check them and view the conclusions through the lens of your knowledge of the context once more. If your conclusion seems way off what you know to be true of the rest of the service or data, go back through your steps from this process and examine the raw data to ensure there's nothing which is giving you an incorrect picture of the situation. Also talk through your conclusions and how you came to them with colleagues who understand the context of your institution, if not to ensure they come to a similar conclusion from all the same information, then at least to solidify your arguments for yourself.

68   DATA-DRIVEN DECISIONS

When drawing conclusions, thinking of them as arguments will help you make sure you are confident in reaching them. You need to be able to explain and understand why your data is saying this particular thing rather than something else. Forming an argument for (and against) this will ensure you are happy with this conclusion.

Exploratory conclusions

Once you collect data for some time and have a wide range of it and a more extensive map you can begin viewing it outside your specific data needs. To draw exploratory conclusions take the same approach as before, however in this instance, instead of being led by your data need, focus more generally on all the different data you have. This is where developing a larger map of data for your service is a real help. A big map pulls together a variety of information allowing you to see different links and relationships between the data. Equally by building up a strong map with a variety of data sources you can respond to new data needs, questions and situations as they arise, putting you in a stronger position within your organisation to deal with changes and the need for change.

The benefit of reaching exploratory conclusions is that it's the only way to find out potential areas for improvement or real strengths in your service without being led by your current preconceptions and knowledge. By drawing exploratory conclusions you can find out entirely new things about your service and therefore reach new and stronger conclusions.

Exploratory conclusions can often fall down the list of priorities so make sure you dedicate time for them. Think about adding a few days once a quarter or a few times a year to focus on a general exploration and analysis of your data, as this will help get you into a habit.

Summary

Making your analysis and drawing conclusions is an involved piece of work, but with all the preparatory steps you have taken you will be sure to gain valuable insights from your data. More than anything, analysing and drawing conclusions from your data is about you and your knowledge and expertise. If you have followed the steps and tips laid out in this and previous chapters, you really are the last piece in the puzzle. As ever, it never hurts to get other perspectives and share your ideas, and you will (and should) be learning and questioning all the time, but be confident in your skills and your understanding and you will be fine.

7 Step 5: Act

Introduction

The hard work for this step was done in the last chapter when you identified your conclusions. We will spend most of this chapter focusing on how you can actually put those conclusions into action and ensure your data and findings are put to good use.

The main topics we will cover in this chapter are:

- making plans and executing developments (page 69)
- sharing findings (page 70)
- trial and review (page 74).

What is the action step?

The action step is simply putting in place what is required to do the things you identified in your conclusions. If your analysis was identifying what's happening, and your conclusion was deciding what you needed to do about it, your action is then actually doing it. This might seem like an easy chapter. Alas, there are many factors which can make action difficult and barriers can arise. With this chapter I'm hoping to help you be aware of them and have some tools to get around them.

Let's start with the biggest question: why do we need to decide and execute actions after completing the process of collecting and analysing data? While it is nice to collect data and understand your service better, it is nothing more than nice if we don't commit ourselves to doing something with the data and enhanced understanding. In many ways data collection without any plan to action in some form wastes staff resources. You need to collect some data over a long period before you can draw on it to make any actions, and you may

70   DATA-DRIVEN DECISIONS

need other data (e.g. from SCONUL, the Society of College, National and University Libraries) for wider statistical inputs. Equally, after studying data you have collected you may conclude that no action needs to be taken at this time – this is still good use of the data (and is in itself still an action – choosing to remain in a certain approach for a period of time). Be vigilant against falling into the trap of collecting data, knowing that your data is telling you there is need for change and then not making any changes.

Actioning is making a conscious decision and plan about what to do with the information you now have about your service and the changes needed to make to improve or maintain this service. It is also the step where we share data, to propose changes at a senior level, to get feedback on proposed changes or to inform and influence colleagues across your institution. Finally, and most importantly, in this step you act and make decisions based on the data. Hello data-driven decision making, we've come full circle.

Sharing data

Sharing data is a key part of the actioning phase of this process for a variety of reasons:

- Very few of us are accountable only to ourselves, and sharing our findings and proposed actions is often a key step to ensuring that actions can be implemented.
- Even if you are in a position to make the final decision to implement actions, you need to be able to articulate your plans, reasoning and general understanding gained from the data to peers, senior colleagues and other colleagues at all levels.
- There will be times where your findings and proposed actions will require more support or resources than you currently have, so being able to share your data and sell your needs appropriately and convincingly is a vital skill to moving forward with your actions.

Report writing

One of the most effective and likely ways to share data is in written reports. There are many things to avoid and much to get wrong when starting writing reports based on your data and findings for the first time so we have broken this section down into a few key topics to assist you when report writing.

STEP 5: ACT   71

Purpose

Before you start writing any report be clear what the purpose of it is, as this will feed heavily into how you approach your writing and the content. Is your report simply to share gained knowledge? Is it to announce intentions of developments? Is it to springboard a conversation into wider developments? It is very difficult to write a report that covers all of these purposes well, so knowing this right at the beginning is really important. For example, if your intention is to share general knowledge then you need not focus on actions and plans, unlike if you were announcing proposals for developments when these would be a core part of your report.

Identify who the audience of your report is likely to be. What time will readers likely have to give to the report and what pressures and interests will they have? If you are passing the report to a head of service, for example, it's likely that they won't have huge amounts of time to read it in detail. Give a strong summary, keep it brief and focus on visualisations over text descriptions to make it more likely that the report is read in full and wins favour.

Defining the purpose of your report will also help to ensure that you aren't spending hours on a piece of work which might not be read or used. For example, writing annual reports can be an excellent time to reflect and show progress or areas of concern, however if there is no formal process around how to action the report or where it is used and who will read it, writing a 20-page report probably isn't a good use of your time.

Make your data palatable and understandable

Writing a report is a standard way to explain and explore your data and actions, however in today's increasingly busy world, people rarely have time to read long reports. Be aware of this when attempting to use your report to influence and inform. Your data might be the most important thing in the world to you, but to someone else it's another thing to think about, so make your reports as easy as possible to understand and as quick a task as possible to read.

One of the best things you can do to make a report easier and quicker to read is to use visualisations wherever appropriate and refer to them in the report. As you considered while mapping your data, using good and easy-to-understand visualisations is vitally important to ensure that readers understand your report and draw correct conclusions from it, so make sure your graphs make sense to other people in the context of the report.

72   DATA-DRIVEN DECISIONS

Length

As a general rule, regardless of the purpose of the report or who your audience is, the shorter the length the better. While sometimes detailed reports are needed, short reports are usually easier to understand (when written well!), to refer back to, and to get people to engage with. A tip for any length report is to make use of a one-page summary. Start every report with a single page with all of the key findings, graphs and conclusions or actions. This way if you ever need to get someone to read your report who struggles with time or who is less inclined to engage, there is a short and easy way in for them.

Layout

Before starting a report have a distinct structure and plan in mind, which should help you write clearly and succinctly. Always start with a summary page listing your actions and key findings, use the core of the report to give details of the data you have used and how it led to your findings, along with any key context that informed the conclusions. Finally reiterate your findings and look more closely at your conclusions and recommendations, and any actions you aim to take.

Writing the report

Your writing should have a clear narrative and story. You aren't simply explaining every piece of data you have collected in this report; you are trying to lead the reader to the same conclusions you have come to.

You don't need to talk through every single piece of information you uncovered in your research. Instead, show the key data and summaries that helped you reach your conclusions and drill down to more detailed data when you feel more background will help strengthen and solidify your narrative. Add context as appropriate with visualisations to strengthen your argument, but again it is not necessary to give every single detail on anomalies at certain dates and so on. Link to your full data map and raw data so readers can explore in depth any areas they want to know more about. Remember that a report does not replace you and your knowledge. Anyone reading the report can come to you and discuss your findings or ask questions; the report does not have to encompass all your wealth of knowledge and answer all potential queries arising from it.

Planning actions

Naturally a big part of the act step in the process is executing (or actioning) your plans on the basis of all the work you have undertaken until this point. We don't ever just go from having an action in mind to seeing the action play out. Taking time to plan properly is the best way to ensure you fully understand your actions and their impact, and you are taking the best approach towards implementing your action. This could have a significant impact on the success of your actions later.

Remind yourself what your action is. You should have drawn your conclusions in the last step – analyse – which will inform what you are going to action, but take the time to understand your conclusions and the different actions which are needed to fulfil the needs identified in your conclusions. Your conclusion will rarely only have just one change that needs to be actioned. For example, if you need to increase the staffing for shelving at a certain period you may need to move staff from elsewhere. The beauty of mapping and drawing conclusions from multifaceted data sources is that we can gain the most accurate conclusions to action, but we also need to remain aware and vigilant of multiple impacts and steps needed in the actioning process.

Project planning

Approaching the implementation of your actions as a project can help to ensure you act effectively and help make your actions work better and become integrated quickly into daily working practices.

Even the smallest actions taken from your data-driven decisions approach need accurate planning. Though it may not be necessary to work through the steps outlined below for every single action, they should give a good framework for putting these actions into place.

Break down your action

First, break down your action into steps to complete to put your action in place.

An example of an action broken into its facets might be that you are going to move items from one collection into a different collection and physical location. This requires supplementary actions:

- create space in the new location
- change catalogue records

74   DATA-DRIVEN DECISIONS

- liaise with staff and students
- reduce the empty space in the original collection
- carry out other preparatory collection work (such as weeding).

You may then need to undertake additional planning to manage one or more of these actions, where further activities would arise. Work through them all until you have a set of clear and individual actions to implement.

Prioritise

Once you have identified the separate actions, prioritise them – high, medium and low – according to their importance for the completion of the project. Though all the actions need to be completed to achieve your final goal, prioritising them helps you to organise and focus on what resources and time needs to be given to each one, and the order in which to approach them.

Plan effectively

When you have prioritised individual actions, order and organise them. There are many approaches to time and project management, but one of the most useful tools to use to help plan effectively is a Gantt chart – a visualisation of your tasks, giving the dates and periods by which they need to be completed. Gantt charts can help outline plans to colleagues and teams, setting out tasks and who is responsible for completing them. See Figure 7.1 for an example.

An alternative is to use project planning and managing software; the key thing is that you find a way to plan, organise and implement your actions effectively.

Trial, review and change

As with any project or change, it's important that you work trials and reviews into your planning. As covered in Chapter 4, ensure you have carved out time to trial, reflect, review and make changes. The same principles are needed here.

The difference when implementing actions is that your approach to trialling depends on the action you are dealing with. Regardless of your approach to your trial and review you should have an extensive enough trial period to be confident that you have the most efficient approach.

Don't forget that as part of your trial and review it is vital to get staff feedback and work with them to plan any changes. This will encourage them

STEP 5: ACT   75

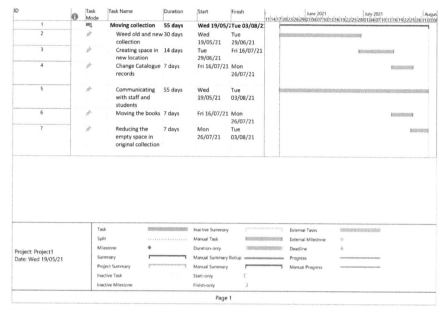

Figure 7.1   *Example of a Gantt chart*

to help you implement your actions effectively and support you if you have to make potentially difficult changes. Staff won't always agree with the changes you are implementing but involving them can have a huge impact on their understanding and the immediate success of the changes you put in place.

Summary

Being committed to making changes and decisions based on your data is the core reason for collecting it. All of the steps until this point take a lot of learning, staff time and resources, and the action step is the key to making all this effort worth it. For actioning and communicating, your biggest tool is forward and effective planning, so take your time.

8 Step 6: Review

Introduction

The main topics we will cover in this chapter are:

- why we review (page 77)
- how to review (page 78)
- implementing changes (page 80)
- what next (page 82).

Why do we review?

At the beginning of the book you may remember all the steps on the lovely circle of the data-driven decision model (Figure 2.1). The circle is one of the most important aspects of the data-driven decision model, and this approach in particular. We aren't simply putting in place a set of processes; we're committing to continuously reviewing and questioning these processes (and putting in new processes). The circular approach is fundamental to ensuring that you are genuinely able to make the most of your move towards data-driven decision making, and creating an ongoing culture of service development. Without committing to reviewing and starting the process again we can easily fall into the well-known trap of not using our data, collecting unnecessary data, and missing out on opportunities to improve efficiency and automation.

The act of reviewing is vital to ensuring you take the most strategic approach to your service delivery and plans. During your review you may find uncomfortable truths about your processes and that there is a lot of work to be done. However, you can't be afraid to face these facts head on and sometimes start again when necessary. If your processes, data or approaches are not working for your service, team and strategy then make a change. That's exactly what your review is for.

What do we review?

Essentially, we need to review any and all practices related to your data-driven decision processes. From how you collect your data, to new technologies available, to how you use your data – it all needs to go under the review lens. Depending on how embedded data-driven decision making is in your organisation and how long you have had your processes in place, it likely isn't going to be a small task. Therefore treat it like an annual project; either review various facets of the process throughout the year or tackle it all at once in a dedicated space of time. Who has the time to dedicate to this I hear you ask? If you take the time to plan your review and approach you can find many ways to save time and to incorporate the review into current processes. Regardless of the time it requires, the step is necessary to reap the ongoing benefits of making data-driven decisions.

How to review and questions to explore

Reviewing is the act of taking a step back and looking at your data-driven decision processes and needs with a critical and unclouded eye. This can be particularly difficult to do, especially if you have spent a lot of time and effort putting these processes together and getting them to work in the first place, but change is inevitable, and that change can and does have an impact on your beautifully drawn-up processes and the data you have selected. If you ever struggle to remove yourself from the work you have done, remember that change happens and it's not your fault, and it certainly isn't a reflection of the work you have done until now. If that doesn't work . . . go for a walk? Have a bath? Talk to a friend? Do what you need to do to appreciate that your work is valuable and that change is necessary.

One of the most important elements of your review process is to involve your colleagues. Include those actively involved in the processes (such as collecting data) and those from other teams who may have different and helpful perspectives to you on how you can improve. Getting staff feedback and involving them in the review process will give you the fullest picture of the situation, help you gain additional insights and enable you to share out the work for the review. There is no set way to involve staff in reviews, and you will know the best way to engage with your colleagues, but the key thing is that you give space for open feedback.

Questions to ask

As with most steps in this book how you decide to approach your review will depend on your specific situation, but there are some helpful questions you can ask yourself to lead you in the right direction and focus your review.

> We use these questions as part of your formal review, but having them in mind while working with data and outside your formal review step can help you hugely when formally reviewing. Consider making a document or space to store your ongoing feedback and answers to these questions, so you have a place to reflect on the regular challenges or issues you come across over time.

Are you using the data and is it effective?

This is probably the most important question you can ask. We've covered the cardinal sin of collecting data and not using or having a plan for it, and while no one would aim to do this it does happen despite our best intentions. Rather than just assume you are using your data and using it effectively, look through your data and highlight when you have used the data and what consequence having that data has had on your plans for the service or your understanding. This line of questioning is also your chance to think about any gaps in your data. Again, look back through how you have used data, what reports you have been using it in, and any noticeable issues you had in analysing it because of lack of data and then implement any new data collection needed from this.

Is your data collection as efficient and effective as possible?

To answer this question, look at the time it is currently taking to collect your different data and then examine how smooth the process is. For example, you could have aspects of the task logged for a period of time to monitor them. Also look at new software, updates to current software, and any new equipment you have in place which could be used to improve or reduce the work required in your data collection processes. Staff feedback and ideas are vital to fully review this question. Your staff are your main asset so use them!

Look at your data collection processes as a big picture. If you have implemented any new data collection processes since your last review, reflect again on whether the newer processes can be combined with previous processes to make a more efficient and simple process. Equally does the introduction of any of your new software or options make it possible to combine the processes now?

80 DATA-DRIVEN DECISIONS

Finally, consider any changes to the wider service of space which may have affected the efficiency or options for your data collection. For example, have there been any changes to space, service hours or anything else which could affect your data collection?

Is the data stored in the best possible way?

Look at how you store your data, how easy it is to access, and review and reflect on how your storage is working and any new opportunities which may make storage easier.

These questions should give you a good framework to start thinking about areas for improvement and how you might identify them. Now take these questions and frame them in the context of the entire process again. This will give you a set approach to re-examining your processes, and help you identify new areas to work on and areas to change within your review.

Make the changes

Once you have reviewed your processes and decisions and given your data-driven decision-making approach a critical eye, you should have some set goals and actions to put into place. When you have an established approach to data-driven decision making, and have methods and processes in place, be careful in how you approach implementing any changes to them. Any changes you make once a data process is established will impact the long-term use and usability of your data, so planning the changes is key.

Here are a few things to consider: the impact of changes on your data, the importance of trials, tell the story and give changes time to bed in, which we discuss below.

The impact of changes on your data

Once you have an established data-driven decision process in place and set ways for collecting and storing your data, handle changes carefully if you want to avoid inadvertently causing problems for yourself later on. For any changes you make to what is collected, where your data is stored, or what your data is called (to name a few examples) you will influence how the data can be analysed if you don't update sensitively to the current process.

For example, if when analysing it you change the name of one of your pieces of data (say 'printer' to 'MFD' [multifunctional device]), it will look as if you have a small amount of data on printers and MFDs rather than giving a full overview of the data, so any changes you make need then to be addressed in the old data. You are essentially using your normalising skills again here but with the new data in mind. Another example is if you change the layout of your data (either by swapping columns or adding or decreasing columns, for example) this can affect how your data is exported or analysed. Reviewing data includes archiving data with old language, or if you are using a system, removing old data and reuploading so it is up to date and not misleading. The main thing is that you can trust the data that you are going to use and analyse, and that it is as clear as possible what the story of the data is.

A warning – never (ever, ever, ever) delete the data you ultimately normalise. You can remove it from your system if you use a system to collect and analyse your data, and create a new set of data with the normalisations in place, but the original data needs to be stored. Remove it from anywhere where it can be confused and name it extremely clearly (something like '*do not use, very old not normalised data*' will probably do the trick), but keep it somewhere.

Trial, trial again

Trialling your new approaches is a fundamental aspect of putting your changes in place as part of your review. We've covered trialling across this book and the same principles apply here. The key difference is to compare the benefits and efficiencies of your new approach with your old approach. Commit to a certain period of time for this trialling and perform the trial as you collect current data and in a separate dataset. This way you won't have any gaps in data while you develop and hone your approach. Equally don't normalise your data until you have had your trials and decided how to move forward.

Tell the story

If it's your job to ensure the journey of the data remains on a single course, it's also your responsibility to document this journey along with any twists, changes or bumps that come up on the road. By documenting effectively, you can ensure that others in future will understand the data, and not make mistakes when using it later. Just as

Ah the story of your data – it's a nice idea, so let's run with it. Your data has taken a journey to get where it is ' today, and that journey never ends. Sometimes your data might change direction, take a side road, loop back on itself. It's your job as the data gatekeeper (mistress, master, hero, take your pick) to ensure that whatever direction your data takes, it always remains on one clear path. Make sure that any time your data may split off into two journeys you bring it back together and document this process so that future data gatekeepers can follow and understand the journey too.

82   DATA-DRIVEN DECISIONS

you have with the processes until now, document all changes, noting where data is stored, dates of changes, details of changes and so on. Write down essential changes of any kind and all their details. It helps to create a document specifically for the history of your data, but you can also include notes wherever possible in the raw data to back this information up.

Give it time

Finally, just as you did right at the beginning of this process, allow change (entirely new implementations and changes to things already in place) time to bed in. Embedding new processes can be tough, but changing well established processes can take even longer as you are untraining and starting fresh. Again, when allowing processes time to bed in, monitor and document any issues that arise, but if you have trialled them and you are confident in your plan, your processes will get back to their normal levels of efficiency in no time.

What next?

There you have it – the end of our toolkit! Alas it doesn't end here though. By this point you have done some amazing work to implement the data-driven decision process and start your path towards a culture of making data-driven decisions, but the journey continues. From here you start right back at the beginning and review any new data needs you have and complete the cycle over again. Soon it will become second nature, and you will start to find that elusive balance between completing the cycle on the basis of specific needs and completing the cycle at set periods of time to ensure you are moving forward. Just give yourself time, and find a rhythm that makes the cycle work for you.

PART 3
Going Further

9 Moving from a Transactional to a Transformational Service Using Data

Helen Rimmer

Introduction

Good data can be one of the most powerful tools for a leader in developing and protecting the people and service they lead. This chapter focuses on data for leading people and will draw on personal experiences of creating a compassionate data-driven service. In the chapter I will illustrate why data is important, how it can be used, and why using data for management and a compassionate culture are not mutually exclusive. Finally, we will explore how to bring your colleagues with you in developing a data-driven culture.

Why lead with data?

Managers tend to have a certain degree of intuition about their service. They know what areas are operating beyond their expectations, whether a particular team is going above and beyond or if a team is just about doing enough and never more. Unfortunately, though, their bosses can't share this 'gut' feeling and it often can't be communicated.

Being able to use data to illustrate what your team is doing can be far more powerful than saying 'my team is busy and we need more staff' or 'students are asking for a particular resource'. Data speaks to power in their language of benchmarking, cost analysis and usage statistics. However, it needs to be the right data. For example, when discussing how busy a team is it is more useful and meaningful to capture all the time taken rather than share only the volume of headline tasks.

More than anything, though, leading with data ensures that you make the right decisions. Intuition is subjective and can favour those who speak out loudest over the people quietly going about their work. Use your gut to push you in new directions but data will verify if your gut instinct is actually right

86   DATA-DRIVEN DECISIONS

and help you understand your service better. In essence, data takes away some of the subjectivity of the decision process and encourages fairness.

Transactional vs transformational work

The idea of transactional versus transformational leadership has been around since James MacGregor Burns described these styles of leadership in his book *Leadership* (Burns, 1978) and it isn't only management styles that can be seen as transactional or transformational. The daily work of colleagues in our teams is also often one or the other, or a combination of both. The transactional work of administration such as book ordering or shelving is balanced with the transformational work of answering a query at the desk, supporting a student with their literature search, or negotiating a price for a journal.

It is important that when teams have a balance of transactional and transformational work this is captured. Transactional work is often easy to quantify through data such as number of books ordered or shelved. The time taken to do it can also be captured, but transformational work is harder to quantify and therefore can appear to people outside your service to take place in staff's spare time. It can also be hard to encourage teams to value their transformational time if data isn't available. However, this data *can* be captured. By using a customer relationship management system, or similar, we can record transformational tasks such as the time taken to prepare teaching or recording who colleagues are e-mailing and meeting. This information can then be used to demonstrate the true breadth of work by teams or to encourage them to value the time spent on these tasks.

Data-led culture

Some people embrace a data-led culture, others are sceptics. It is essential you try and win over the sceptics, even if some are hard to convince.

I have introduced data-driven services and combined transactional and transformational data twice. The first time (in Library 1) was easy; there was a lot of trust and crucially there had been a lot of data used over the previous few years so bringing data front and centre was painless. The second time (in Library 2) was much more challenging and staff a lot less trusting.

Staff in Library 1 were used to using data; they had recently been through a large development project where data of different types had informed decisions on layout, staffing and design. They understood how to use data. Crucially, staff had seen colleagues defend the service using data produced daily and used in meetings, reports and conversations. The move to be a fully data-driven service and capturing everything transformational and transactional was fairly painless as they trusted management, already used data and knew that the new data captured would fill obvious gaps.

Staff in Library 2 were more threatened by the introduction of data capture. They felt they were being spied on and shouldn't have to capture the more transformational information. Interestingly, some staff preferred to focus on transactional tasks because they could use data on the number of books ordered or reading lists completed to argue that they were busy. On the other hand they were much less keen to collect transformational data.

With hindsight I should have been more subtle when introducing a data-driven service at Library 2, encouraging use of data daily for activities such as rota planning and resource purchasing before looking at people and time.

As discussed in the toolkit, alongside collecting more data to create a data-led culture it is important as a leader to actually use data yourself and to choose the data you are requesting carefully. After all, nobody likes to be asked to collect data that isn't used or has no purpose, and if you are struggling to help people understand the benefits of a data-led culture this is a key element to get right at the beginning. Though we had some serious sceptics in Library 2, as I knew exactly why we needed particular data and showed how I would use it I was able to bring some of them on board.

Data champions

Whether you are in a service that is comfortable with data, or you have a very anti data service, one of the best things you can do is identify your data champions. These are staff who are interested or excited by data and are engaging early on. It's important that you nurture these staff in every team, and bring them along in your vision and on your journey. They will be invaluable in supporting the rest of their colleagues through the transition into a data-led culture and will be some of your strongest assets in this process.

Identifying data personalities in the team

In their article 'Who's afraid of data-driven management?' Bladt and Filbin (2014) describe different types of employee by level of regard and performance, and level of engagement with data. These are their headings and my personal experience of working with people who fit into them:

88   DATA-DRIVEN DECISIONS

1 *Highly regarded, high performing* These staff members are often sceptical or simply non-interested as they have very little to prove. They are already highly regarded and their performance supports this high regard. There is a risk that any data collected doesn't truly reflect all the hidden work they do and this will alienate them. If they are engaged early on and involved in decision making over what data is collected then they can often become champions as the data adds to their high regard.

2 *Highly regarded, low performing* Bladt and Filbin describe these employees as the hardest to convert and argue there is little that can be done with this group. They are already well regarded but data may uncover their lack of performance and so they have very little to gain from embracing a data-driven culture. If people aren't doing anything data gives them nowhere to hide no matter how highly regarded they are. This can scare colleagues under this heading and they could fight the process as their position and power may be threatened. However, in my experience these staff can be won round if they are shown something positive about the data rather than it being only used as a performance management tool. It can open up conversations about training, development and workload, However, long-term low performance inevitably leads to performance management and data can support this process too (looking at trends, not the minutiae of what staff do on a specific day).

3 *Lowly regarded, high performing* This group should love collecting data as it gives them the recognition of their outputs which they may have been lacking despite working hard. It can be surprising when you look at data and realise how much some people do under the radar. This is the strength of data over intuition. Ensure you recognise this group's high performance and they will champion data greatly.

4 *Lowly regarded, low performing* This group will either go with a data-led culture (and improve their performance) once they realise that this is the new normal, or they will push back but not raise their performance, and come under no pressure to do so. They are the most likely to leave a data-led service because of the culture change and no longer being able to hide their lack of performance.

Understanding and knowing how these types of colleagues fit into your teams is important to change the culture. If you can identify types 1 and 3 and really engage them to begin with, the work of bringing about a compassionate data-driven culture will become easier. You will also have some champions who can support the shift in opinion of types 2 and 4. It is useful to keep these categories in mind to understand the reasons for resistance to data; some

MOVING FROM A TRANSACTIONAL TO A TRANSFORMATIONAL SERVICE   89

people who fall into type 1 could turn into a Type 2 if their high performance isn't acknowledged.

Data with compassion

At times data can be painted as cold and hard, uncompassionate and not compatible with a compassionate management style. However, if you are a compassionate manager then it follows that you will use data compassionately. After all, there is nothing more compassionate than a service where everybody is working smartly, with sustainable workloads and to the best of their skills.

It is vital that data is not used for micromanaging. Don't look at what an individual does on a specific day or week, but rather at trends over time and over teams. If you want to build trust and really use data to build your service this point cannot be stressed enough.

In my experience teams function better when everyone pulls their weight. Often if one or two members of a team aren't doing their fair share of the work, even if those team members are highly regarded, it is picked up by the rest of the team. This results in the team stretching to do their own work while covering for the low performing team member. Once the team is rebalanced to ensure everyone is doing a fair amount, the productivity and quality of the work increases. Those carrying the low performing colleagues will feel the relief of a reduced workload.

Importantly, this data will also allow compassionate conversations around why a low performing colleague isn't doing as much as the other members of the team – is there a fear factor or capability issue? You can then explore solutions using the data. For example, are there particular tasks which play to their strengths? If they are very good at developing marketing materials can they take the lead on that and relieve the rest of the team of that pressure?

Here are some tips for building a compassionate data-driven service:

- Use data as a leader. When you make a decision, back it up with data and always ask for data from your teams. This is the core principle of the toolkit at the start of this book, but it's always worth a reminder.
- Ensure you use data to give insights and create actions. Show why you are asking for it and what added value it gives by committing to your action step of the toolkit. For example, you may know how many calls you get to your live chat but how can you use that data to improve the customer experience? You could look at what queries can be turned into frequently asked questions (FAQs) or become a focus for training. Or are

90 DATA-DRIVEN DECISIONS

there often queries about a particular aspect of the library catalogue? If so then use data to push for change.

- Acknowledge the uncertainties in the data. Where there could be errors, can they be mitigated against? This is where your documentation, expertise and use of context from the toolkit is vital.
- Nurture the data enthusiasts on your team.
- Use existing data to look at what data can be obtained through existing systems with little user input, make this data easily available through a dashboard or regular reporting using the mapping stage of the toolkit.
- Use data to reward and understand your team.
- Encourage the use of data internally, enabling colleagues to become data literate and see the importance of data for themselves.
- Train your team on how to use data, on potential errors in statistics and looking at the bigger picture. This book can be used to give a common language and understanding to your team, which can be invaluable when creating a truly data-led service and not leaving less confident people behind.
- Use data to inform process reviews. Automate transactional tasks and add value to everyone's work along with improving the user experience through quicker response times or delivery of materials.
- Ensure that your data is consistent across the service. Agree what data should be collected by all teams to provide a baseline. It is useless if different teams record data differently.

Case study

Background

Data is powerful. In one of my previous roles we had a liaison team who were generally highly regarded and perceived to be high performing. They had already made good use of data without direction. Indeed, they used to improve the timing of teaching by looking at data on 1-2-1 tutorials and ensuring they offered targeted teaching and advocacy connected to where there had been trends in what was being asked. They also used data extensively in content and collection management, so they trusted and understood its importance.

It was clear that some of the work of the team had changed over time and the balance across them all needed tweaking. This combined with a new vacancy made it a good time to review the team and how they worked. There was a sense that restructuring may be coming with decisions made externally to the library service. This included possibly not recruiting to the vacancy in

MOVING FROM A TRANSACTIONAL TO A TRANSFORMATIONAL SERVICE   91

the team. Thus work to restructure and review the team would be looked on favourably by those making the overall decisions.

Data collected

To begin with we had data collected on the core liaison work, broken down by department under these headings for that academic year:

- teaching hours (not including 1-2-1s) – self reported
- total hours 1-2-1s – self reported
- number of orders – from the LMS and spreadsheet used for nonstandard orders
- e-mails: student – self reported; departmental staff – self reported
- student numbers, undergraduate (UG) and postgraduate (PG) – taken from the LMS
- number of postgraduate researchers – taken from central data
- calls in the enquiry management system (EMS) – taken from the EMS.

Table 9.1 shows the breakdown across the team.

Table 9.1   *Breakdown of data collected by five liaison librarians in case study*

Current distribution of load	Teaching hours (excluding 1-2-1s)	1-2-1 hours	Orders	Student e-mails	Staff e-mails	Student numbers (UG and PG)	Post-graduate research-ers	Calls in EMS
Liaison librarian 1	33.2	19	3106	98	577	2210	258	69
Liaison librarian 2	32.8	27.25	6928	146	282	2168	108	35
Liaison librarian 3	29.5	7.5	6936	107	213	1811	202	48
Liaison librarian 4	53.25	9.25	3700	96	269	2309	126	48
Liaison librarian 5	54.8	50.9	3392	381	813	3111	162	94

Table 9.2 on the next page shows a snapshot of the highest statistics in each subject.

92 DATA-DRIVEN DECISIONS

Table 9.2 *Breakdown of data collected in case study showing highest statistics in six subjects*

Current distribution of load	Teaching hours (excluding 1-2-1s)	1-2-1 hours	Orders	Student e-mails	Staff e-mails	Student numbers (UG and PG)	Post-graduate research-ers	Calls in EMS
Biological science	16.5	0.5	495	26	169	612	75	21
English	6.45	6	3569	53	99	788	47	17
Geography	16.25	1.75	1132	34	135	618	49	30
Law and criminology	16.3	36.05	1766	185	243	656	25	10
Management	24	11.85	760	106	372	1707	70	40
Psychology	14.5	3	866	90	198	748	67	44

The balance of work within the liaison team

As you can see from these tables each librarian had differing balances of work. Using data from Table 9.1 we found that those with high teaching loads tended to have subjects which needed fewer individual books to be ordered. The aim of using this data was to help inform the balance of subject liaison and to understand how librarians could support several subjects. To do this we needed to use the data in Table 9.2 as a base and then look into further similarities between subjects, for example, which referencing system was used, which subjects were combined in dual honours degrees, etc.

What this data told us

Liaison Librarian 5 had the highest teaching load, highest number of 1-2-1s, most calls in the EMS and a large number of e-mails from students and staff. They also had the largest body of students to support. Conversely Liaison Librarian 3 had a low teaching load, low number of 1-2-1s, relatively low numbers of e-mails and the lowest number of students but the highest number of book orders. Book orders fall into the transactional work of liaison rather than transformational work. It was often purchasing from a list and at the time budgets were high and there was very little need for transformational intervention such as negotiation or finding out-of-print books (this was reflected in the more detailed notes field). The data showed that the remaining three librarians' workloads fell somewhere between those of these two in balance.

The data on ordering allowed work to take place on streamlining the ordering process and decoupling the routine orders from the liaison team, leaving them free to liaise over such things as availability of resources or length of reading lists. Overall the team was spending 64 hours on book ordering, which is the equivalent of 1.83 weeks of 1 FTE person's time over the year. If this could be reduced, then the team could focus on the more transformational liaison work around collection development.

It was clear that the traditional way of dividing subjects between the team by either student numbers or amount of teaching was not a fair indicator of workload.

The non-core liaison work

We knew that there was a lot of other work going on, so we looked at other data available which showed the time spent on various tasks over a six-month period from December to June (as we had started data collection in December, ideally we would have had a full year). There were 72 different categories of task across the service. Table 9.3 shows the tasks that the liaison team spent most of their time on, by broad category; it is not exhaustive.

When the time taken on all these tasks was allocated to each liaison librarian it became clear that some were taking on far more additional work than others (Table 9.4, next page).

Table 9.3 *Tasks the liaison team spent most of their time on in case study, by broad area*

Content management	Enquiry management	Engagement and outreach	Staffing	Admin
Data analysis and reporting	E-mail (not in EMS)	Academic liaison	Meetings: university	Analytics and reporting
Ordering: books (all)	Enquiry management system	Library guide updates	Meetings: external	Event organisation
Ordering: electronic	Helpdesk	Library induction	Meetings: library staff	Planning
Reading list maintenance	In person	Postgraduate support	Professional development	Project work
Weeding and disposal	Live chat	Reading list advocacy	Recruitment	Report or document writing
	Phone	School visit	Team activities	
		Social media	Training	
			Training prep	

94   DATA-DRIVEN DECISIONS

Table 9.4 *Time liaison librarians spent on 'non-core' tasks each week in case study*

Librarian	Time spent on 'non-core' tasks throughout case study (6 months)
Liaison Librarian 1	94
Liaison Librarian 2	209
Liaison Librarian 3	292.5
Liaison Librarian 4	38.4
Liaison Librarian 5	181

Identifying the roles in the team

This work showed that Liaison Librarian 3 would have fallen into the low regard or high performing category as they quietly got on with their work, performing very highly and undertaking vital extra tasks such as a stock project, marketing and events. However, Liaison Librarian 4 who was doing a lot of teaching wasn't doing much beyond their core tasks. This data opened up conversations around what the team enjoyed, what they felt was their role and what the service and university needed from them in future.

Looking at the data we found that some areas, including transactional tasks such as reading list management and dealing with e-mails, stood out as taking up a lot of time. Liaison Librarian 3 spent 17.75 hours on 368 e-mails inside and outside the EMS. It was decided this could be managed better with all e-mails going through the EMS and simple queries which didn't need their expertise being answered instead by the exceptional team of information assistants. The more detailed queries could then be passed to the liaison librarian or, in their absence, to another liaison librarian. Under the current system if liaison librarians had been on leave then the e-mails sent directly to a particular librarian would not have been answered until they returned.

Table 9.5 opposite shows the highest amount of time liaison librarians spent in each overall category.

The story the data told

Some of these figures were surprising, for example, the amount of time liaison librarians spent in meetings with other library staff (including team meetings) was almost 6 weeks of 1 FTE over a 26-week period. When we looked across the whole service it was clear that some meetings were more vital and useful than others. We started holding team meetings monthly instead of weekly, sometimes calling specifically focused meetings in between. We thought about whether it was necessary for several people from one team to attend

Table 9.5 *Highest amount of time liaison librarians spent on tasks in case study, by category*

Overall category	Time spent on all tasks (total hours over 6 months)	Heading with most time spent	Time spent (total hours over 6 months)
Content management	273.82	Reading list management	154.71
Enquiry management	307.45	E-mail (not EMS)	174.11
Engagement and outreach	448.74	Academic liaison	142.38
Staffing (e.g. meetings, professional development and recruitment)	698.9	Meetings with other library staff	208.96
Admin	306.1	Project work	90.88

the same meeting, and whether the number of staff attending the meeting could be reduced. This was a good example of something which we knew in our gut was an issue but quantifying the time spent and translating it into the FTE equivalent helped push through the change needed.

Process reviews, discussions and actions

Once we undertook process reviews and discussed expectations around the role of liaison librarians we concluded that we could redistribute the subjects. In discussion we broke down what the role of liaison was into transactional and transformational tasks, asking the team to identify what they thought fell into each category and what they thought could be done differently. Some suggested there should be more automation of the ordering process and importantly that we start training information assistants in liaison work. This would allow them to answer basic enquiries and improve the customer service at the desk by allowing information assistants to respond to frequently asked questions without reference back to the liaison team. The team also used the data to look at patterns in 1-2-1s and queries to advocate for teaching sessions connected to specific assignments and areas of the curriculum.

It was also very important to differentiate between reading list maintenance and reading list advocacy. The team was spending a lot of time on maintaining the lists but didn't have time to their contacts to get more people to engage with the system or to discuss the age-old question 'what is a reading list?'. To solve this we revised the process for reviewing lists and engaged more people with the admin of the list process. This allowed the liaison team to focus on where their skills were best used by advocating for reading lists. As a result the academic body started to understand what

DATA-DRIVEN DECISIONS

students and the library needed from the lists and the work on the list admin became more valuable as the lists were more useful to the students.

Conclusion

All our discussions, backed up by the data we had collected, demonstrated that liaison librarians did not purely carry out core tasks, but used their expertise in project work, wider training and engagement. We also discussed their own professional development as part of the review, identifying which tasks it was useful for liaison librarians to have competence in to help them move into other roles (project work and line management stood out).

We modelled various structures, including what would happen if we lost a post and a scenario where we created a role with a focus on online teaching and less subject-based work. This helped to demonstrate why the data we had collected was so necessary.

Throughout our review the team were involved in creating data and discussing their roles. The work we undertook to show the breadth of the work done in the team also persuaded our management to fill the vacant post as we were able to quantify how much work a new liaison librarian would do.

The review worked because:

- it rewarded the high performing members of the team with increased recognition
- there was a feeling of fairness in the reallocation of tasks and expectation that all should be involved in project work or marketing, and so on
- the team were involved from the start in the data collection process.

10 Collection Mapping for Collection Management

Amy Stubbing

Introduction

Using data effectively is a vital aspect of the collection management umbrella. One of the nicest things about using data for collection management is that you are already likely to have access to a lot of readily available data. If you are confident in pulling data from your LMS (or have someone with whom you can work closely to get the relevant data) you can draw information on what materials you have, what subject they're in, their usage, and location, and more. This strong base of available data can be coupled with additional information from outside sources for more in-depth understanding and decision making for collection and stock management. When harnessed effectively this data can have a significant impact on your collection management practices, collection strategies and stock management practices.

Moving towards data-driven collection and stock management has a variety of benefits. Effective and creative uses of data can enable you to:

- create effective processes for stock and collection management
- plan collection development within the actual needs of the service and institution
- understand your collection and align it with institutional needs
- identify the strengths and weaknesses of your collection.

In Chapter 10 we explore how collection mapping can be used to enhance your understanding and direct your plans for your collection. Collection mapping will help to develop your decision making and should support the development or change of collection development policies and approaches.

Understanding your collection as a concept

We start the chapter by considering your collection as an abstract concept, which isn't nearly as difficult to understand (or explain) as it sounds. The concept of your collection is the overall idea and quality that your collection encompasses. It is essentially the purpose, strengths and direction of your collection. In identifying these things, we can better understand our collection and how it will be used in the future, plan high-level decisions for its development or control, and tie it into wider institutional strategies. One of the most important aspects of really understanding your collection as a concept and these different facets is that you then have a set of guidelines which you can compare your collection against over time to measure its performance. How well your collection is used is after all only one small facet of really understanding how valuable and relevant it is.

Nailing down the purpose, strengths and direction of your collection requires a lot of information to be pulled from different sources and then examined together. Let's not forget just how important looking at your data is in context, and without oodles of context you simply cannot confidently or fully understand your collection. The process of pulling together all of this information is called collection mapping, which is what we will focus on for the rest of the chapter.

Collection mapping

Collection mapping is a constantly developing approach which has seen many iterations and focuses over the years. There is no one way to undertake collection mapping, and the specific parameters and approach will be defined by the needs and purpose of the exercise in any given institution.

The goal of a collection mapping exercise is to be able to write a report which defines your collection as a concept and most importantly outlines actions based on this information. When undertaking a collection mapping project you need to follow the themes of the toolkit, and as we now know, *all projects should lead to clear actions*.

For this chapter we will focus on university library collections, however the principles are transferable to any library. As with everything to do with data there are a huge number of variables which change depending on the situation within your institution, so chop and change this approach based on your specific needs.

Plan your collection mapping project

As we know from earlier in the book, always start a data project by identifying

COLLECTION MAPPING FOR COLLECTION MANAGEMENT 99

what you need to know and what you need the data for. In collection mapping your goals are to:

- find out about your collection (or understand it)
- categorise your collection
- draw up an action plan for your collection.

As you work through the stages of collection mapping and each of these goals follow those same principles outlined in the toolkit. You should be able to highlight which part of the toolkit you are working through at each stage and use this knowledge to ensure you are not missing any core steps.

What is involved in each of these goals?

Understand your collection

The process of understanding your collection is the first step in collection mapping and must be completed so you can categorise and create actions for it. What you need to find out depends on your situation and the context of your library collection so you will likely need to add to this list.

What is in your collection?

First ask what is actually in your collection. This base of understanding will form the context for your wider analysis looking at strengths, weaknesses, usage and so on later on.

Now I realise that 'finding out what is in your collection' is an extremely vague ask. Start by looking at broad categories: break your collection down into facets. Things to identify are different collections (collections of maps, scores, oversized books), different material types (books, journals, CDs, maps, scores), how many titles you have in each subject area compared with the number of copies, whether there is any uncatalogued stock, and any other general areas.

When you boil this step down you are essentially giving the background to your collection and highlighting any potential areas of interest so you are aware of them when completing the next stages.

What are your collection's strengths and weaknesses?

Identifying the strengths and weaknesses of your collection requires you to gather a range of data from different sources, but before you get to that at least have an idea of what constitutes a strength or weakness in this context. This view may change somewhat when you have all of the data, but there should be some fundamentals you can assume for your institutional context and strategies. For example, having an old collection may be a strength for libraries in certain subject areas with a research focus, whereas an old collection for a library focusing on the sciences would (largely) be considered a weakness.

Defining the overall rarity and uniqueness of your collection is a good way of benchmarking against other universities and finding out which of its areas have value to the wider sector. This is useful when defining your strengths and value internally within your organisation, and can also help important collection development decision making. Rarity does not necessarily equate to value for every institution, especially if the collection does not align with your wider institutional goals.

To identify the rarity and uniqueness of your collection you need a source of data to compare against. For universities in the UK, the Jisc Library Hub Compare tool (https://compare.libraryhub.jisc.ac.uk) is likely the most comprehensive database to use (previous iterations were the National Bibliographic Knowledgebase project and the Copac Collection Management project). For this kind of database you simply need to upload your collection data to compare it with other libraries that are part of the database, allowing you to find out what percentage of your collection is held solely by your library, or is rarely held. You can use this information to find out the overall strength and rarity of individual facets of your collection (e.g. your philosophy collection).

When using these kinds of databases you can upload all your data to get an overall picture, but it is worth breaking it down into specific collections to support your analysis later on, so keep this in mind.

As with all data for collection management, look out for potential errors or red herrings. Databases for comparing collections are only as good as the data put into them, so look out for anomalies such as hardback copies and paperback copies being identified as unique, or data errors which can falsely flag unique items. (This is where your review step from the toolkit comes in!)

How does the collection meet research and teaching needs?

Being able to identify how a university library collection correlates to the specific teaching and research needs of the institution is a key way to identify its strengths and weaknesses. The first thing you need to know is what the strategy of your university is towards teaching and research – is it heavily teaching focused, heavily research focused, or an equal split? The next step is to identify how much your collection is supporting research and teaching respectively.

One of the most comprehensive ways to identify how your collection correlates to teaching needs is to compare your collection to reading list data. A good way to start your analysis is to examine what proportion of your stock is on reading lists. This allows you to identify how much of your collection is actively used for teaching and how much is (in theory) more research-based material. Naturally this analysis will depend on how your institution uses reading lists, so the analysis and conclusions you can draw will depend on the set-up you have.

You can take this analysis a step further by examining how often individual titles appear on reading lists and comparing the figure with the number of copies per title you have. Thus you can find out how teaching needs are reflected across the different areas of your collection, any areas of particular strength, and any outliers.

Using the data gained from looking at reading lists, you will be able to get (in theory) a percentage of the number of items that are teaching focused (on reading lists) and which are research focused. For example, if 30% of items from your collection are on reading lists it suggests that 70% of items support research.

To identify how your collection aligns with the research focuses of your institution find out what the institution's research outputs are. Examine the repository where your institution stores research outputs. If you are in the UK, using what was submitted for the Research Excellence Framework (REF) is a helpful way to define your search, but you may need to include more recent data if there hasn't been a recent REF review. For this work it's good to define what will be included, for example, remove non-research-related outputs (such as book reviews).

Consider these points when identifying research outputs:

- Research outputs can vary widely in type and size (most commonly journal articles, chapters and books), but there are many other formats which are still considered research outputs to include and consider.
- Be aware of the different sizes of departments and the impact this has on your data (remember to normalise your data).
- University research changes all the time depending on staff turnaround, funding and so on.

To compare your collection against research outputs, map the research outputs to your library classification system to make the two comparable. This probably has to be done manually if it is to be accurate. Luckily you don't need to drill down to the exact classification. If you are using Dewey classify up to the decimal.

102   DATA-DRIVEN DECISIONS

Classifying your institution's research outputs is a simple but often time-consuming process, so you need a range of staff comfortable enough in specific subject areas to support this part of the project. To classify, download the relevant information (such as research title, subject, author's department) and then classify based on this information. It is not a foolproof method but it gives a good indication of how the research outputs map against the classification for comparison.

Once you have completed the classification work you can then compare the focus on research with the focus of your collection. This can then be cross-examined with the reading list work you have probably already completed to identify any areas of your collection which do not map to teaching or research focus (allowing you to confidently identify areas of strength and weakness).

At this point think again about the context of your library and institution. This work won't highlight any upcoming research focus for the institution, for example, so keep things like this in mind. Equally, if you know a subject is not going to be taught or researched in future, this needs to be part of your conclusions.

What age is your collection?

Once you understand the focus of the institution that your library sits in you can begin to examine and analyse the age of your collection. As mentioned above, the age of your collection can be a strength and a weakness depending on the situation and needs of your institution.

To identify the age of your collection it is helpful to break it down into manageable areas and chunks. One of the simplest ways to do this is to use your classification system as a base. If you use Dewey you can look at the age of the collection by the top-level classification (000, 100 and so on), then drill down further into areas of interest, areas which have different requirements, and areas for potential concern after your initial analysis.

Identify the criteria that you are measuring against; your criteria may be 'published in the last two years', 'published two to five years ago', 'published five to ten years ago', 'more than ten years ago' or 'over 100 years ago' (for example). As ever, the criteria depend on the context of your library and what you need to know. Include a range of levels and options so that you can find potential issues or strengths along with actions (e.g. if your science collection is largely five to ten years old this might be a problem or suggest that it needs to be weeded).

COLLECTION MAPPING FOR COLLECTION MANAGEMENT 103

How is your collection used?

A pivotal part of understanding your collection is to look at it how it is used. The usage data required for collection mapping is more detailed than figures simply highlighting loan statistics. To gain a full understanding of how your collection is used, and what its value is to users (along with its strengths and weaknesses within this context), identify your user groups and determine how you expect them to use the collection. If you are in a university your user groups may be broken down by level of study for students, staff, and what subject users are studying. You can use this initial data along with information gleaned from calculating how your collection supports teaching and research to map how users draw on different sections of the collection. Compare your total teaching and research users against your teaching and research collection sizes.

The next step is to map the subject areas of your institution against your library classification system. This is not an exact art but will enable you to compare data and draw a detailed analysis when mapping your collection against your institutional needs. Table 10.1 shows an example of subject areas of a university library mapped to the corresponding Dewey area.

Table 10.1 *Subject areas of a university library mapped to the corresponding Dewey area*

Dewey number	Dewey area	Subject area		
0	Computer science, information & general works	Computer science	Electronic engineering	
100	Philosophy & psychology	Psychology		
200	Religion	Religious studies	PPE	
300	Social sciences	Economics	PPE	
400	Language	French	German	Hispanic studies
500	Natural sciences and mathematics	Biological sciences	Earth sciences	Maths
600	Technology	Management	Electronic engineering	Physics
700	The arts; fine & decorative arts	Drama, theatre and dance	Media arts	Music
800	Literature & rhetoric	English	French	German
900	History & geography	Classics	Geography	History

With the data from mapping the subject areas of your institution against your library classification system you can identify what aspects of the collection you expect specific users to engage with and compare them with usage data. Knowing how widely your collection is used is a good way to understand its impact and significance on a larger scale than individual subject usage. Equally you can find out what areas of your collection specific departments engage with. This will allow you to make more detailed decisions about and even influence how you manage collection development as a whole.

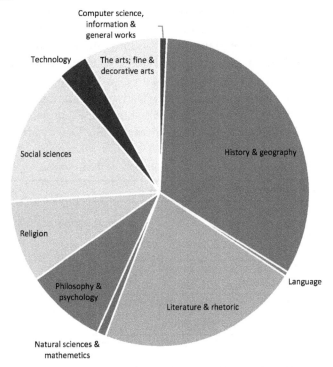

Figure 10.1 *Undergraduate and postgraduate classical civilisations loans by Dewey area*

How much are you spending on your collection?

To understand your collection find out how much you spend on it and in what areas. Ideally your spending should map institutional needs and be reflected in your usage statistics, research outputs or institutional strategies (e.g. whether you have a research or teaching focus as an institution). As with all other aspects of the collection mapping work, make your data and analyses comparable, so consider examining your spending based on your library classification system as a place to start.

You can also examine spend on different collections to compare the cost of resources and the amount of resources gained for your money in each area. This is helpful when planning budgets and advocating the specific needs of each collection. By using this data alongside the wider picture you gain from collection mapping, you can make decisions on collection development and identify instances where your current practice does not map the needs of the institution or service.

Categorise your collection

The ultimate goal in collection mapping is to use your understanding of the collection and compare the information you've gained about your collection with the purpose of your collection to inform your strategic approach and decision making. The next step therefore is to consider how you understand your collection in the context of your institution and its purpose. This understanding can inform the purpose and context of your collection, but these should largely be defined by institutional strategies and teaching and research outputs.

A practical way of ensuring that your collection aligns with the required purpose and context from your institution is to categorise the different parts of the collection. For this determine how you want the collection to develop, for example, do you want it to grow, do you need to reduce it, does it have value, doesn't need to be developed but should not be disposed of, and so on. Once you have listed your criteria, group them into categories.

For example, Royal Holloway Library undertook a collection mapping project. This library service supports teaching and research, has a special collection and collections of historical value, and a collection with areas that are no longer relevant to the institutional goals. Royal Holloway Library staff created the following categories for the stock:

- *flagship*: areas of high research and/or teaching interest, where collection development is a priority and collections can be expected to grow
- *heritage*: areas where stock is of research and/or teaching value but where collection development is not a priority and where collections are expected to remain static
- *current*: areas where stock has current research and/or teaching interest but is of limited long-term interest (e.g. text books, reference works)
- *finite*: areas of low research and/or teaching interest (e.g. subjects previously taught or researched, but not currently), where collection development and maintenance or renewal is of low priority.

106 DATA-DRIVEN DECISIONS

Once you have defined your categories create the criteria for a collection that fits into them. Table 10.2 shows how three criteria fit into four categories.

Table 10.2 *How three criteria for individual titles fit into the four categories flagship, heritage, current and finite*

Criteria for title	Flagship	Flagship	Flagship	Flagship	Heritage	Current	Finite
On reading list	✓	✓	X	✓	X	✓	✓
Aligns with research outputs	✓	✓	✓	✓	X	✓	X
Rare	✓	X	✓	✓	✓	X	X

Create an action plan

Categorise your collection and plan appropriate actions based on your criteria. With this work completed you should have a clear plan of how you are engaging with different parts of your collection (e.g. targeted engagement for flagship collections, weeding or rehoming of finite collections) and how it will develop in future.

Conclusion

Collection mapping is a significant project and needs to be undertaken with the right amount of resources, and a lot of passion. While it is a big undertaking, it truly is one of the most transformative data projects you can complete.

Once you have completed the tasks laid out above, you will be armed with real knowledge and a confident direction for your collection and its management. How you move forward from here is really down to you. You could plan a multiyear project to address issues in the collection. You might begin collecting in a new area. You could even plan bigger changes to how your collection is organised. Anything is possible and nothing should be ruled out when you get insights from projects like these!

11 User Experience and Qualitative Data

Emilia Brzozowska-Szczecina

Introduction

In this chapter we will explore a key tool in data-driven decisions: user experience. Over the next few pages we will learn about:

- UX research and how it can help you
- UX techniques and which best help in answering your questions
- recruiting participants and ensuring your research is conducted ethically
- analysing data
- deciding what to do with your data
- things I wish I knew before I started my first UX project!

What is UX?

As you may have guessed, UX is just the abbreviation of user experience. We pronounce it as 'yoo – aex'. But what is UX? 'User experience' is simply how someone feels about using a product or service (Schmidt and Etches, 2014, 1). In our case – how our library users feel about the services provided by our library.

UX has its roots in ethnography as its methods (such as observations, interviews or cognitive mapping) are used by ethnographers, anthropologists and many other specialists in related disciplines. It is especially prominent in web and applications design, unsurprisingly because big companies such as Facebook or Google want their apps to be as innovative, tempting and attractive to their users as possible.

In the SCONUL report *Mapping the Future of Academic Libraries*, UX was recognised as the fifth critically important library skill next to strategic and relationship management, and understanding the research process and

108   DATA-DRIVEN DECISIONS

negotiations (Pinfield, Cox and Rutter, 2017, 44). Wherever there is a product or service, there are clients and users too, and the goal is to make the products or services useful and attractive, so users will want it and will come back for more. Needless to say, it is worth investing your time to learn about it!

The four stages of UX

The UX research and design process should ideally have four stages:

- Discover: plan and conduct research.
- Define the data analysis and generate ideas.
- Develop ideas into actions and develop a pilot or prototype of a service or a product.
- Deliver: launch the final version of the product or service (Priestner, 2020, 3).

Undertaking UX research in a library

We all want our libraries to be the best they can be, and to be functional, with satisfied, frequently visiting users, but as with other data gathering processes discussed in this book – for UX you need to have a good think and identify what you want to find out. Additionally, have a good think if you, your colleagues, and management *are ready* find out. Remember: the UX research method will give the voice to users, who will not always tell you what you expect, and what they tell you may not always be complimentary. You can be sure however that data obtained through UX research will give you a great evidence base for bringing a positive change to your library (if it is needed).

Below I will present some core techniques of UX research along with guidance and suggestions for when you can use them, and some useful tips on recruitment of participants and research ethics.

These are just my suggestions, so please do feel free to explore this field further. UX research (and design too) loves creativity. You can absolutely mix methods if you feel it will be helpful in your case, or even change the methods. This kind of research is a perfect way of finding answers to the questions we did not even know we want to ask.

The UX techniques

Before we look at specific techniques, there are some crucial things to keep in mind:

USER EXPERIENCE AND QUALITATIVE DATA 109

- Whatever equipment you use for recording – ask the participant if they agree. Check 'Ethics of research' (page 117) for more information.
- Don't attempt these techniques entirely alone; use your colleagues and their perspectives.
- Always allow extra time in the project to recruit participants and analyse results – see 'Recruiting participants' (page 118) and 'Analysis' (page 119).
- If possible, carve out some money in the budget for incentives – see 'Recruiting participants' (page 118).

We discuss seven techniques for undertaking UX research: cognitive mapping, touchstone tours, web usability testing, observation, focus groups, interviews and cultural probes. To help you build up your experience and make an informed decision on where to start they are scored by level of difficulty:

- easy (might consist of just one question or task to do)
- moderate (slightly more preparation from you is required, perhaps to prepare some questions)
- difficult (requires more knowledge, preparation and complex analysis).

Cognitive mapping

Cognitive mapping is very simple and effective. A cognitive map is a user-drawn map of a library (or a university campus, a building in which the library is located and so on). Drawing this type of map usually takes no longer than six minutes so it gives a great picture of how the participant perceives the library, and which points and elements of the services are most critical.

Good for: checking if the library building is functional and/or meets the needs of library users, finding the way in your building is easy, library users are aware of a service or a facility available in the library.

Difficulty: Easy.

Time needed: Each meeting with a participant takes around 15 minutes; you can do it over 1–2 weeks.

Shopping list: Sheets of paper, three colour pencils.

How: Ask the participant to draw a map of the library (or a selected space in the library, a school building or university campus). Either:

- allow users 6 (or 15) minutes to draw a map with one colour OR
- give them three colours, for example, start with green, then switch to red after 2 minutes and then switch to black after another two minutes (or switch colours every 5 minutes if doing it for 15 minutes total).

110 DATA-DRIVEN DECISIONS

In the second technique the pen colours can show what the participant thought about first when drawing the map, and highlights what could be more important for them (Priestner, 2018a).

In both cases, once participants have finished, ask them to talk you through the map and note down their comments.

Analysis: See 'Visual analysis' (page 120) and 'Affinity mapping' (page 121) later in this chapter.

Note: Think about asking additional questions once the map is drawn. This technique works better with users who are at least vaguely familiar with the library.

Touchstone tours

You are probably used to giving library tours to users, but this time library users give *you* the tour! They take you through the places and spots that are essential from their point of view. This simple and highly effective technique works great with first time users or visitors and shows you how easy (or not) it is for them to find their way around the library.

Good for: checking if the library building is functional and/or meets the needs of library users, and if finding the way in your building is easy.

Difficulty: Easy.

Time needed: Each meeting with a participant depends on how big your library is: 10–30 minutes should be sufficient.

Shopping list: Just a notepad for you. You could also use a smartphone to record the video, take pictures or record the video during the tour.

How: Meet participant (who may or may not have visited your library before) at the entrance door to the library or building where the library is located. Ask them to walk you around the library telling you where they usually go and in which order, or if they have never visited the library before to show you the most obvious route. Ask them to find the way around the library with some tasks in mind – perhaps looking for a good study space, finding a computer or borrowing a book. Ask them to think aloud and comment as you walk together. This is a perfect method to discover how users find their way, to observe user behaviour and in general discover how participants feel about the library.

Analysis: See 'Visual analysis' (page 120) and 'Affinity mapping' (page 121) later in this chapter.

Web usability testing

A library user tests the library website or discovery tools by performing a set of tasks.

Good for: checking if the library website and/or discover tools meet the needs of library users, and if your website and discovery tools are accessible or easy to use.

Difficulty: Difficult (but worth it!).

Time needed: Each meeting with a participant may take 15–60 minutes. You can do it with other colleagues over 2 weeks.

Shopping list: A computer, laptop or tablet (one if you sit in same room as participant, two if you conduct the testing remotely), software for online meetings with screen capturing and recording (record the screen and audio for these sessions for the analysis).

How: Ask participant to perform a couple of tasks related to the areas you want to check (e.g. find the library website, use library catalogue, find out the opening hours, request a book, or access an online resource) commenting aloud while performing the tasks. Tell them that there are no wrong answers, and this is not a test of their abilities or knowledge about the library. Think well which tasks you want to prepare beforehand and ensure you keep a completion score, which will be important later in analysing this data. Make notes during the testing. Watch the recording later and make notes or transcribe what the participant said. Ask colleagues to watch and make notes too if possible to ensure you pick up as much as possible.

Analysis: Check 'Free text analysis' (page 119) and 'Affinity mapping' (page 121).

Observations

These are observations of spaces in the library, made with a printed floor plan of that space. An observer marks the occupied spaces and users on the floor plans, as well as other elements: activities, routes, equipment used or noise levels. You can observe at some crucial times of the day – morning, lunchtime, evening – or just once per day, depending on what you are trying to find out.

Good for: reviewing use of reading rooms or study spaces, zoning in the library, functionality of facilities and furniture, layout of the library.

Difficulty: Difficult.

Time needed: One observation should take around 20 minutes and be conducted during a working week (5–7 days depending on the opening hours of library).

Shopping list: Pencils or pens, printed plans (A3 or A4) of library with an added grid to mark all the sitting spaces, matching clipboard (A3 or A4).

112 DATA-DRIVEN DECISIONS

How: Observe the chosen area for approximately 20 minutes and mark the taken study spaces showing each user in an occupied space with 'x'. You can add symbols for noise levels (e.g. 1 for quiet, 2 for some moderate noise or quiet conversation, 3 for loud); activities (e.g. R for reading, T for talking, S for sleeping, E for eating, H for hogged space); and/or for object being used (e.g. L for library laptops, O for own laptops, B for book, F for food). Add objects to your observation if

> **Pro tip**: Check when head-counts are taken in your library. Your observation will provide the user numbers occupying library space at that time anyway, so you can help colleagues and spare them the effort of taking the headcount at the exact same time when you are observing.

useful for checking if the library laptops are used in the library or taken outside, if allowed; or if the books are ever used in the library when borrowed. Finding out the level of other activities such as eating or hanging out may help you justify making changes such as increasing social space for users, especially if you have lots of users who commute. It can also help to establish if library zoning works well and if some facilities are more popular than others.

Note any significant comments on the other side of the sheet – but be careful only to include those of significance so as not to overwhelm yourself with too much data. Depending on your type of library, you can conduct this research two or more times during the year to compare the usage.

In Figure 11.1 opposite you can see an example of a heatmap made using Heatmapper (www.heatmapper.ca) – a free tool for data visualisation. Colours depict the number of people, showing which spaces are the most popular. You can apply heatmap to present the noise levels as well.

Analysis: Check 'Free text analysis' (page 119) for the comments and 'Affinity mapping' (page 121).

Focus groups

A focus group is a meeting with a group of people where a moderated conversation takes place. The moderator guides the conversation by asking questions prepared beforehand so participants can have their say about the discussed topics – the library services or some elements of it.

Good for: reviewing any element of the library services before planning any new developments.

Difficulty: Moderate.

Time needed: Takes the least time of all the methods presented here. A discussion for a single focus group may take 40–60 minutes. The timing can be flexible; just make sure it is not too short, so participants have time to say

USER EXPERIENCE AND QUALITATIVE DATA 113

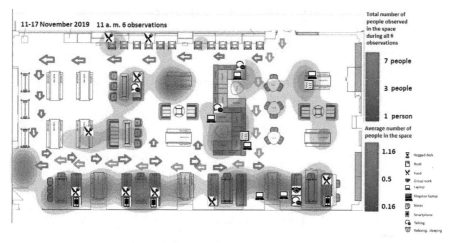

Figure 11.1 *Observations made daily for a week at 11 a.m. in the silent study area of Kingston Hill Library, Kingston University London*

something. People may agree to give you an hour of their time – don't let focus groups run for more than 90 minutes.

Shopping list: Video and voice recording device – can be a smartphone.

How: Focus groups can take place face to face in a room or online, using software for online meetings. It is useful to have a colleague with you, to help you start the discussion. Focus groups can be difficult to run as you need to moderate the conversation skilfully, but remember that participants have agreed to take part, so it is very likely that they already have something in mind that they want to tell you or at least are ready to contribute. Have something on hand to say about the discussed topic (or prepare presentation or printed plans). Put as many open questions as possible. Try not to let one person dominate the conversation and encourage everyone to have their say. Sometimes sharing your experience about the discussed library topic can help too!

Ideally have between five and eight participants. If you recruit more – congratulations – but make sure everyone has a chance to speak. If you end up with just two people, do not worry. Recruiting participants is tough, but the game is far from lost. Consider if it would be worth interviewing each of them (see 'Interviews', immediately below).

Analysis: Check 'Free text analysis' (page 119).

Interviews

Interviewees answer questions prepared beforehand about your library services (or some elements of them).

114 DATA-DRIVEN DECISIONS

Good for: reviewing any element of library services, before planning new developments.

Difficulty: Moderate.

Time needed: 10–30 minutes.

Shopping list: Voice recording device (can be your smartphone) or notepad.

How: Many UX techniques that require participants to complete tasks include some form of interview, which should have a natural flow as the task is performed. However, if you are only holding an interview, think ahead about questions on the topic you are researching (as with focus groups); consider asking a colleague to look at your questions with a fresh pair of eyes; and if possible hold a mock interview to test the responses to your questions.

As when conducting focus groups, try to make the questions open and remember that if participants agreed to be interviewed they are willing to talk to you, so let them speak. Give the floor to the user. The less you speak, the better – it is all about them, so listen. Ideally the participant should speak for 80% of the time while you spend just 20% of the time asking questions (Priestner, 2018b).

> Interviews and focus groups are great and can give you lots of precious information but be careful! There is something about being put on the spot – many people will give you not the real answer to your question, but the correct one. People often have the best intentions in their minds by telling you not what they really do or know, but what they think is expected from them to do or know. And this is not what we are looking for! Any activity requiring the library user to perform a task (drawing a map, taking you for a tour) without any prompts from you is more likely to show you the raw reality of how your library and its services are functioning from their perspective.

If your interviewee has trouble giving answers, you could ask them to describe something factual, for example, about the time when they first enrolled in the library. Try to make it casual and make sure that the participant knows that you appreciate their responses.

Depending on what you are researching, having even five interviews completed will help. I do not recommend going beyond 15 – it is a lot of data to analyse! Each interview gives you a lot of insight if you choose a diverse group of participants.

Analysis: See 'Free text analysis' (page 119).

Cultural probes

Good for: the library experience of a particular group of users or UX in a specific period.

USER EXPERIENCE AND QUALITATIVE DATA   115

Difficulty: Difficult.

Time needed: One week or more for participants to complete tasks.

Shopping list: Notebooks; set of coloured pens, pens (can be ballpoint); blank postcards; emoji stickers; printed plans of the library, campus or building where the library is located. Setting up some online space to upload photos from participants will help, envelopes for each task, tote bags or boxes, perhaps some sweet snack or other item tailored to the task.

How: First, think about the topic. As this is the perfect technique to research various elements of your library in one place, it may be worth narrowing down the group of library users. For example, I was involved in a cultural probe to check how new students experience the library and university campus during their first weeks in collaboration with the Campus Life team, who organised all the events during the Freshers Week (Phillips and Brzozowska-Szczecina, 2020).

Accessibility: Ensure attendees know that people of any ability are welcome in writing, drawing or taking photos. If writing a diary is not possible consider voice recording. Is there someone in your community who could help translate for non-English speakers? Inclusivity is essential and will give you a picture of the library drawn in many colours and shades.

Taking pictures and drawing: Think about the tasks you want to include in your probe. This can be drawing a postcard from your local town or first day at the campus, taking photos of some significant places, objects or moments (e.g. your favourite place in the local town or the library, what is important to you, what gets you through the day and so on).

The 'map task': Take a map (of your local area, campus) or library plan and ask participants to stick emoji stickers (available online) on it picturing how they feel about particular areas as they visit them – cheerful, sad or angry; just make sure the emojis are free of profanities! Or simply ask participants to draw or make notes on the map, but doing this exercise using emoji stickers simplifies the process of recording reactions later.

The 'diary tasks': Use a diary (can be a simple exercise book) with prewritten questions carefully created and chosen by you to get the desired insight. Ask participants to describe their first visit to the library, the first time they joined a workshop or class, attended library induction, borrowed a book or accessed an e-book from the library – if they have not undertaken any of these activities yet, prompt them to do so and then describe how it went. Think about the order of the questions – first ask about the visit to the campus (or local area), then the library and then borrowing a book and so on. Plan cultural probes to last two weeks, so you can comfortably ask five to six questions. Your choice depends on what you are trying to achieve but don't go for too many

116 DATA-DRIVEN DECISIONS

– remember participants have other things to do. Give them an additional week or two after the probe finishes so they have time to complete the task.

Follow it up: It may be very useful to conduct follow up interviews with participants once the tasks are finished. Encourage them to tell you stories and gain additional insights. Once the research project is completed, consider scanning the results of the cultural probe and giving them to the participants – it may be a nice keepsake for them from that time in their life!

Analysis: See 'Free text analysis' (page 119), 'Visual analysis' (page 120) and 'Affinity mapping' (page 121).

Other methods

These are some other UX techniques to try:

- *Behavioural mapping:* Take a pack of coloured pens and observe a chosen library space for 20 minutes. You can perform one or three (morning/midday/evening to have a picture of how your library is functioning during different times of the day) observations per day for one week. Choose one colour for each user and draw an arrow as the user moves around the library. Add notes on a separate sheet if required. Once the task is completed, compare all the sheets, and analyse your comments. Remember: can be tricky to analyse.
- *Graffiti wall:* The simplest method there is! All you need is a blackboard to write on or a wall in your library where you can put Post-it Notes (provided by you beforehand). Ask a question on the 'graffiti wall' and ask library users to reply on a Post-it Note. Keep questions simple, for example, 'what do you think about . . . ', 'what is you first impression of . . . '. Check the wall regularly (in case there are any profanities – even cheerful).
- *Love or break-up letters:* This fun method encourages users to write a love or break-up letter to a product or service; the tone will depend on how they feel about it. My colleagues and I mixed this method with a graffiti wall – it was divided into two parts so students could write how they felt about the academic library building which we knew would close before we moved into a new building. The outcome was amazing – we had poems, funny and moving letters, rants – all written in several languages (students and staff helped enormously with the translation).

Ethics of research

It is important to carry out UX research in an ethical manner, especially if you require library users to take an active part in it. First check how your organisation handles the kind of project you are planning. Higher education or research institutions are likely to have a research ethics committee or its equivalent in place, whose staff can deal with your questions and advise you on what documentation and processes to put in place before you start recruiting participants. Some organisations may require you to submit a brief description of what you will be doing, and ask participants to sign a simple agreement form or even just confirm by e-mail that they understand how the data arising from the research will be used, and

> **Pro tip**: UK Data Service (2021) has very useful guidance. Check it to find out how to inform participants about gathering data during a research project, and how the data will be used and stored. There is also a very handy template of an informed consent form, for participants to sign as a proof of their formal agreement that you can gather and use the data (video and voice recordings, diaries, taken pictures for the cultural probe) from the project.

agree that you can gather it. Others may ask you to fill in a lengthy application with a lot of details describing how the data will be gathered, stored and used.

Anonymise data

It is important to anonymise the data arising from the research project and not to gather any sensitive data about participants. Read the General Data Protection Regulation guidelines of your institution. Remember to assure participants that their data will be anonymised, and personal details will be accessed only by you and any staff involved in the projects, and preferably deleted once the project is finished and contact with the participants is no longer needed. However, you may be required to keep anonymised data for as long as ten years depending on your organisation's individual policy.

Whatever output is published, make sure it contains only vague details to differentiate between participants (such as person A, person B), so it would not be possible to identify them.

Assure participants that if they change their minds and decide to withdraw from the project, they can do so without any consequences.

When you don't need complex paperwork

UX research in which users are not taking an active part or when they do so completely anonymously (such as making observations or graffiti walls) does

118 DATA-DRIVEN DECISIONS

not require any complex paperwork. It would however be a good idea to notify library visitors via library social media websites or posters that some research is taking place to see how the library is being used. The presence of a member of library staff with a clipboard can be a little intimidating, so just let people know what is happening.

Recruiting participants

For many of the methods described above, you need to recruit participants from your library users. This is the last step of the preparation, and you can only do this once your management agrees, your colleagues helping you are briefed on the project, any paperwork regarding research ethics is ready, incentives are established, and any necessary equipment has been purchased.

Diversity is key

Try to make the group of participants you are focusing on as diverse as possible. For example, if you are in a higher education institution and want to research how postgraduate students use the library, try to recruit students from the UK and abroad, those who commute and those who live on campus, students with varying needs and studying different courses. Try to include as much diversity as possible to give you much greater insight.

> Be prepared: some of your participants may cancel or not show up. Having a waiting list will help you with planning!

Ways of recruiting participants

Remember to have participant information – what they need to know before they can agree and sign the informed consent – ready when you recruit. These are some of the most popular ways of recruiting participants:

- Produce some simple posters and leaflets.
- Approach library users directly.
- Set up a stall at a local fair or event as a member of library staff.
- Via your library's social media channels – Twitter, Instagram, Facebook. Try to post the request for volunteer participants a few times per week.
- Use an institutional or library newsletter.

> **Pro tip:** Have some booking system in place. Participants can then book on their own at a time convenient for them. You can synchronise available slots with your calendar and set up buffer times in order not to overload you with meetings.

USER EXPERIENCE AND QUALITATIVE DATA   119

- Send communications in your institution's virtual learning environment or shared workspace.
- Use incentives: anything from tickets, gift cards or points towards an extracurricular activities award if you work in an academic library. People will often help you regardless of the prize, but incentives are a nice way to thank people for their help and time.

Analysis

Here are a few methods for analysng the data you will gather by applying the UX research techniques listed earlier on.

Free text analysis

It may seem difficult to analyse free text, but it is simply about reading your data accurately, as well as finding any repeating data pieces and labelling (or coding) them. We are working in the libraries sector, so classification skills may come naturally to many of us.

Deductive vs inductive analysis

There are two main methods of approaching analysis:

- *deductive analysis* (or top down sorting), where you create labels in advance from all your knowledge and experience, then apply them to the data as you read it
- *inductive analysis* (bottom up) where you create labels as you read the data (Campbell Galman, 2016).

My coding is rather inductive; I create my labels as I move forward through my notes and sort the data as the topics are emerging. It works well, especially when you do not know what questions to ask.

The deductive method is like sieving data through the questions you have established before you started your research, but probably the ideal balance is to use a method somewhere in the middle of the two.

Transcribing

Once you have recorded an interview you have to transcribe it, either manually or using speech-to-text tools. If your research is conducted over

120   DATA-DRIVEN DECISIONS

Zoom, MS Teams or similar, then remember the transcription can be done automatically for you, although you may need to check that the words have been captured correctly.

If you have any diaries, notes or Post-it Notes from the graffiti wall, use them. Just remember to scan or copy your originals so you can liberally write on the copy when needed.

Coding

Coding involves sorting data into topics and ideas, perhaps using colourful pens or markers to separate them (this is why you need a copy). Give topics simple names (e.g. 'library induction', 'opening hours', 'facilities') and use sub-sections – 'A', 'B', 'C' – if you wish. Go through your data more than once – have a break between each time you read it. There is always a chance you will notice something new!

Use Excel for analysis

There is also another way of analysing data – enter each section into an Excel document. As any topic emerges, separate the relevant chunk of text, and add your label in the next column. If one line has more than one label, you can copy it. You can use the 'Sort' function to see all the label categories you have created immediately.

Do the maths

Once you are satisfied that you have identified all the topics and labelled as much as possible, you can do the tally. Check how many times each topic appears. If helpful, sort it – this will show you what your library users mention most often. This is where you will use the qualitative analysis skills gained in the toolkit. In this context qualitative analysis can be tricky, as you must use your judgement to decide what is most important. For example, some faulty equipment for library users with special needs may not be mentioned as often as popular but disputable topics, but could be more urgent to bring up with library management for an urgent intervention. What are the problems, gaps or perhaps opportunities?

Visual analysis

You have gathered a nice bunch of cognitive maps or photo studies created religiously for your project by your participants, but what do you do next? Below is my step-by-step guidance for you:

- Print or copy the item you want to analyse. Whether you want to keep things printed or electronic, you need to have a copy, so write on it and keep the original pristine the way your participant handed it in to you.
- Add a sheet to each item. On the sheet add some information about each piece you have – you can number all of them, add the date when the copy was created, and some brief information about your project. In general – keep it tidy and consistent.
- Have a good look at the item, think of any important messages the participant wanted to convey: what are the most prominent elements? Are some parts of the library missing? (This could be important on the cognitive maps of your library.)
- Circle or mark elements you think are important. Whether on paper or on a device, use colour coding if it helps. Make notes, add any thoughts. Identify problems and opportunities.

Use dedicated software to analyse a lot of data: this will work well if you have a lot of data to analyse, so could be useful in some circumstances. Have a good think if the software will actually be fit for purpose. The most popular software is NVivo, which can be expensive, so first check if your institution already has purchased NVivo or its equivalent. There are some open-source software alternatives and some offer a free trial, such as ATLAS, so you can always do some research first on what would be the best option. Good software can help you with transcription, managing coding and referencing. But if all you need to analyse is a transcribed text from ten interviews, then it may be easier to stick to an Excel or Word document. In any case, choose whatever is best for you. I like to analyse my data manually!

Once you have completed these tasks look at the notes. Here comes in the affinity mapping (explained below) or the coding you already learned about in the free text analysis. Sort out the notes and highlighted objects into categories and create codes or labels. Doing it in a table or Excel will help, as it will help you to sort out the data, but if you just like to keep it simple in a Word document, that can work too. Again, you can check what topics or ideas appear most often, as well as what are the most urgent or appealing ones.

Affinity mapping
Affinity mapping is for those who like to work in a group or to approach data

more visually. I recommend it if you do not have a lot of text to analyse, but it can also work with textual analysis. It is the process of creating an affinity diagram by gathering qualitative information and grouping it by category.

Post-it Notes to the rescue

Look at your data – what topics come into your head? Write each of them on a Post-it Note. You can do it together with your colleagues – do not worry if things repeat. Take advantage of various colours. You can categorise your Post-it Notes into problems, behaviours, user groups, facilities and so on (Priestner, 2018c).

Stick the Post-it Notes onto a wall, look at them together with your colleagues, analyse and discuss them and take notes. Try using Padlet or the Whiteboard facility within MS Teams – there are plenty of tools from free and paid software that you can use for this purpose and work on collectively, even if you and colleagues are working remotely.

Now write it up!

Great job, you have gone through the toughest bits! Now you need to find the best way to convey your findings. A report will give the much-needed context for the data and background and offer the directions in which the outcomes of your UX project can be taken further. Keep it simple though. You probably know very well how difficult it is to carve out time and read anything during a workday and the same applies to completing (and reading) your report.

Remember we all have limited time (and energy), so tables, charts, graphs and maps will be more than welcome for any tired colleague or manager. In his chapter 'Reports are boring and you know it' Pshock suggested some helpful tactics to communicate UX research outcomes, such as presentations, blogs, flyers or newsletter updates (2020, 45). These are all great ways of circulating the outcomes of your research, but some institutions still prefer a very formal approach, so sometimes only a good old report will do.

Regardless of what form you choose to present your research, you need a good frame, a skeleton to help you transform your research outcomes into good evidence supporting the need for change or appraising the library services as they are.

For this you can an apply the FRAMES (Focal sentence, Rich description, Analysis, Meaning, Expand and So what now?) model. It puts all the elements of your research into a logical order, and is very versatile. It works well regardless of any form of presentation of research output. Table 11.1 shows the elements of the FRAMES model in tabular form.

Table 11.1 *Elements of the FRAMES model set out as a table, adapted from Campbell Galman (2016)*

Focal sentence	Your key theory at the start of the report. This can be the need to change or improve some library services because of a forthcoming event, as uncovered by your research.
Rich description	How you have conducted the research, why, when and who participated in it, and what kind of data you have gathered.
Analysis	Write up your analysis. How did you analyse the data? Describe the key topics, ideas and patterns.
Meaning	What is the meaning of your findings? What are the problems and opportunities?
Expand	Elaborate on the problems and implications for the library. What solutions do you recommend?
So what now?	What are your further plans? How will you follow up your findings? Are you planning to repeat your research? See This is the beginning (page 125) to find out more.

As you can see, I preferred to explain each of the elements of the FRAMES model in Table 11.1 rather than write it line by line. Many people will agree with me that presenting this information in a table is easier to read – please consider this when you write up your research. If you choose to present your research in a shorter form – a leaflet or a smaller infographic – focus on one problem, and the FRAMES model will still work for you.

If you decide to write a full report, think about writing an abstract of it or an executive summary, where you will give a snapshot of the whole report on one page of A4. Outline the most important things, use bullet points to make it easier to read. Apply similar sections in the summary and the long report, so anyone reading the executive summary will have no problem with finding more detailed information in the main report. Worried that no one will read the whole report? Think about creating a presentation or a blog post if your organisation has one!

What next?

The ideal scenario is to have an opportunity to present the outcomes of your research to the management and the rest of staff, and/or anyone else who is accountable for the area you are researching (e.g. the IT Department). These stakeholders should then consider your recommendations, implement at least some changes, and justify why others could not happen. In the current climate with financial cuts and shift to the remote and digital, it is almost sure that your organisation won't be able to afford all the changes you propose, or not necessarily make them in the way you wish. However, just an acknowledgement that the changes are needed can be the first step towards implementing them in future and may inform future decisions in the area you researched. Make sure your research has not been wasted. Remember, all this work is for library users, and you can use this experience to improve theirs.

As mentioned before, although there may be outcomes from your research that you didn't expect, or comments that are unpleasant to hear, they are likely to be a fraction of the whole feedback. The majority of the feedback will usually consist of positive and rewarding comments or constructive criticism.

How might we solve problems raised in your research?

If you identified some problems in your report (justifying the need for change) and your management gave you a green light to act on them, you again need to gather a group of relevant colleagues. It is great when various teams or departments are represented. Brainstorm together various solutions to address the identified problems. Ask 'How might we . . . ?' to get a discussion going.

For example, your participants mentioned several times that there are always long queues to the helpdesk, but it turns out that not many of them knew about library chat. So ask yourselves 'How might we popularise the use of library chat?' You might get replies like these:

Include it in a library induction for students and/or staff.

Promote it in newsletter, library social media or other channels.

Brief the customer services staff to mention it when responding to an enquiry.

Make it more visible on the website.

Taking each idea further will require working with various people and departments, so someone who can help you to identify a solution or at least to advocate for it will be an asset on your project team. It is great to have a senior manager who supports you and your team's effort to address problems and who is willing to take them to the library's director.

Words of caution

It is easy to get carried away with UX research so be aware of your capacity. UX in libraries is still a new trend – not many institutions have a dedicated UX job post but assign UX research as an additional task to a member of staff who already has other responsibilities.

It can become a big pull on time if you aren't careful. If possible, do not do it alone. Either ask for volunteers to conduct the research or help you analyse the data you produce, or at least make your management aware that you need a lot of time to do this.

Before you even start, make sure your management knows what the UX research is about, and they understand its value and how effective it is in showing users' attitudes and behaviour. Be sure that your managers will consider the outcomes of your research.

This is the beginning

Conducting research and analysis are just the two first stages of the UX research and design process, after which two other stages should happen: develop and deliver. The whole process often finishes after researchers write up the report or discuss the research. Priestner (2020) noted that many librarians struggle to generate ideas owing to obstacles related to organisational culture, institutional politics and in general fear of failure (thus are anxious to voice ideas).

The 'develop' phase of the research process takes the idea generation to the next stage. The solutions we came up with should be then implemented. The feedback is gathered and analysed, the outcomes reported, and the final changes applied. Once the researchers and stakeholders are satisfied, the new version of the product or service is launched (hence this stage being called 'deliver').

Is the project now completed? Well, kind of. But remember in an ideal world, the launch should be followed by more research, thus more changes applied as the time comes, and new feedback emerges. After some time, new users will come, probably with different needs, and new technology or software will be developed. Perhaps some changes in our organisation will occur. And so, we go back to the beginning.

Remember UX research is how we can gather the much-needed evidence for the decision-making process to ensure library products and services will be relevant and desired with the user in mind!

12 Alternative Data Sources: Using Digital and Social Media to Inform Management Decisions in Your Library

Leo Appleton

Introduction

When we think about data in library and information service management terms, we tend to think about facts and statistics relating to library operations. As we saw in the toolkit, quantitative statistics can often be generated through automated systems but can also be gathered through other means such as observation (e.g. physically counting people who are using the library). Libraries also generate an equal amount of qualitative data through asking for feedback about the library, which allows us to gain opinions or perceptions from people. These types of data collection are well embedded in the general performance measurement and continual improvement activities of the library profession. Indeed, the current quality and performance measurement literature provides evidence of this trend (Cervone, 2018).

However, there are many less obvious or newly emerging sources of data that we are yet to harness effectively across the profession. This chapter will look at some slightly different approaches to data collection for library management and, in doing so, will identify several alternative digital sources of data which can be used to inform strategic and operational library management decisions. We begin by looking at how a huge range of library-related data can be obtained through web-based and social media channels and platforms. Then we focus on how such data can be analysed and how library managers can use it in a performance measurement and service development environment.

Libraries and social media

Library and information professionals are no strangers to social media and have made effective use of it now for many years, often being the pacesetters and pioneers for innovative use of social media in a professional capacity. The 2014 white paper 'Use of social media by the library' identified four distinct areas in which libraries use social media in order to operate and engage with users: marketing and promotion, collection management, outreach, teaching and learning. The paper suggests that libraries and librarians were experimenting with social media usage in the mid-2000s, before it became a mainstream tool for library operations (Taylor & Francis, 2014).

Phil Bradley, a well known library and information commentator and social media expert, reflected how he first discovered social media by accident in 2005 and began to collect and collate social media platforms on his website, as he felt that they might be of some use to the information profession. Then within a week, after just one mention on his blog, he was getting 50,000 hits a day. This is when he realised that there was a really large seismic shift in the way that the internet was evolving as a means of generating and disseminating information (Bradley, 2015). This example demonstrates the enthusiasm, uptake and early adoption of social media by information professionals. I certainly recall my own excitement as a further education learning resources manager at discovering Facebook and Twitter in 2007 and thinking how such tools, along with the emerging 'smart' hardware, had the potential to transform how we carried out many library operations.

As change agents and having mastered the move to digital information resources, I would argue that library and information professionals in general were not afraid to try these new technologies out and have continued to make full and effective use of social media platforms ever since. Librarians have been particularly high-profile users of social media for marketing and publicity purposes. Patel and Vyas (2019) identify several such marketing and publicity purposes: to promote events, exhibitions and services; to advertise collections and resources; to highlight subject specific resources; and to promote training and instructional events. Similarly, social media is well used by libraries for intentional engagement activities to connect with existing users and potential non-users, and also with the wider community in which the library is located.

Library and information professionals have also used social media tools to collaborate with colleagues across their institutions, sectors and networks, and have been quick to adopt and include social media and web-based platforms in their library teaching and learning activity. This can include using social media platforms as an information resource and teaching social media literacy.

Social media terminology and background

Before we explore data and social media in more depth, we examine how social media as a concept began and where we are now.

The term social media is still frequently used, and people understand it to mean several different things. For many it refers to tools and platforms such as blogs or wikis, or microblogging platforms such as Twitter, or specific social networks such as Facebook, LinkedIn, Instagram and TikTok. However, the term 'social media' was actually adopted along with the expression 'web 2.0'. This tried to convey the second iteration of the general World Wide Web, when web functionality and control became far more user oriented and where internet users were able to generate web-based content themselves for others to interact with. 'Social media' became the acceptable description for any online platform which allowed users to exchange content, ranging from opinions, news and views to digital objects such as music and video files. However, the current use of social media as a term refers to web 3.0 or even web 4.0, suggesting that the capabilities afforded by the internet and associated connectivity have moved even further on.

The classic 'social media' tools identified above are so called because of the social elements of interaction with others that they afford. However, the web 4.0 world in which we currently live includes many more online collaborative tools which can be used for social and educational interactions, both of which are key to library and information services. As e-citizens we no longer question notions of streaming video and audio, hosting and collaborating in the cloud, or accessing and interacting with our networks via a whole range of apps. Social media and web 2.0 were indeed transformative but web 3.0 and web 4.0 offer library and information services so much more, and this includes access to data.

While I have just suggested that social media is no longer an appropriate term to use when discussing the current digital environment, I will continue to use it. It has longevity and is still meaningful to those who use it, and no doubt it will continue to be used and will continue to mean current collaborative digital platforms.

What sort of data are we talking about?

Much of the literature about libraries and social media focuses on 'engaging with users' and how social media enables this. At a very basic level the simple metrics generated by things such as the number of likes, followers, tweets, retweets, shares (all common parlance in social media terms) can give libraries an idea of the numbers of individuals potentially engaged in their social media platforms. A study conducted in Canadian academic libraries in 2015/16 involved analysing their social media usage data with regard to user engagement and looked specifically at the influence that their social media platforms had over an eight-month period (Winn et al., 2017). This influence was all measured quantitatively through analysing engagement data associated with specific Facebook posts and the number of 'likes' and 'shares' associated with particular posts, and similarly the number of 'likes' and 'retweets' which were generated from particular tweets.

This kind of data is available to all library and information services who want to measure the uptake of their social media and potential user engagement. However, this is only really demonstrating engagement with social media and not necessarily providing data about library operations or engagement with other library services and resources. What libraries really need to do is to be able to use social media data in order to measure engagement with specific strategic outcomes and objectives, such as 'increasing use of a particular resource' or 'increasing attendance at library-based events'. It may well be that a specific social media campaign can contribute to or influence the success of a wider marketing and publicity initiative, and the actual messages, posts and tweets, as referred to above, would invariably be part of such a wider campaign (e.g. to increase resource usage or attendance at events). How do we use the data to inform decisions about these? In order to answer this, it is useful to look in a bit more detail at the different roles that social media plays in library and information marketing and publicity.

Data from social media marketing activity

Marketing is one of the first library management activities in which social media was effectively used and applied across a range of library and information sectors. In the early to mid-2000s when social media emerged, its first and primary use was a social one as a platform on which users could connect and engage with each other (hence the label). However, very quickly, many industries and organisations adopted social media platforms as a channel through which to promote and publicise (and effectively sell) products and services. Commercial marketeers were quick to realise the potential benefit of being in 'mass-market' space and over time social media became a regular platform for marketing and publicity activity. Libraries in the higher and further education sectors were also early adopters of web 2.0 and social media platforms and had begun to use them for similar activity, informing customers about opening hours, collections, resources, exhibitions, and so on, and other library sectors soon followed.

This chapter is about the data that can be generated through social media and digital platforms and used by the library service to inform decisions, not how to use specific platforms or how they can be used for marketing and publicity. Instead we focus on the types of data that might be generated through this activity, and where this fits in with library strategy and operations. However, there is a blurring of these boundaries, in that the data generated from social media marketing activity actually informs library social media marketing activity. To better understand this, it is useful to look at the 'marketing cycle' depicted in Figure 12.1, as identified by Allan (2019, 53).

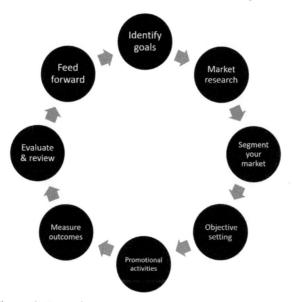

Figure 12.1 *The marketing cycle*

With regard to this marketing cycle, much of the activity that libraries and librarians are involved in is promotional activities. This is the part where marketing messages are delivered and the campaign comes to life, physically (e.g. through posters, flyers, banners, etc.) and digitally (e.g. through digital screens, web pages and social media). There is much literature available celebrating good practice in this particular area, and it will come as no surprise that many case studies share good practice in libraries using social media to full effect in their promotional activities (Potter, 2012; Dryden, 2014; Hicks, 2014). However, from a data perspective, and data-driven decision making in particular, it is the sections of the marketing cycle entitled 'Market research', 'Measure outcomes' and 'Evaluate and review' where social media has the more significant role. In his evaluation of social media presence in libraries and information organisations, Cervone suggests that for social media data to have any value it needs to be able to 'help discover what people want from and care about in relationship to the organisation [and to] understand what is happening in response to our social media messages and provide meaningful information that can be used as evidence in taking action' (2017, 3). In other words, in order for it to lead to decisions being made, social media data needs to inform our market research and our measurement and evaluation respectively.

Social media data for market research

As briefly discussed above, levels of user engagement (or at least engagement with users who use social media) can be evidenced through quantitative 'uptake' data (e.g. likes, likes per tweet, retweets). This is powerful data that informs us of the 'reach' and potential influence of our social media work. However much social media data is qualitative, in so much as it is the narrative found in comments, tweets, replies to tweets, and threads that can provide insight into our library and information users, their perceptions, experiences and expectations. It is here that market research can take place and by engaging library users in dialogue through social media, you can generate really useful and meaningful data. It might be that library users might comment or respond to a piece of publicity, or even comment on areas of library activity that they are happy or unhappy with. In all these instances your library users are telling you a little bit about themselves, their behaviours and their experiences.

In these cases, more sophisticated data analysis techniques are required which effectively takes us into the realms of data science and big data analytics, in particular, especially if you are in the fortunate position of having large amounts of qualitative social media data to analyse. These are some of the key data analysis techniques which are often applied to social media data analysis (Batrinca and Treleaven, 2015):

- natural language processing, the process of a computer extracting meaningful information from natural language input, as you would expect to find in social media outputs

USING DIGITAL AND SOCIAL MEDIA TO INFORM MANAGEMENT DECISIONS   133

- text analytics, which involves studying word frequency distributions, pattern recognition and tagging
- sentiment analysis, which brings together natural language processing and text analytics in order to identify and extract subjective information in source materials, such as social media.

This type of social media data analysis is likely to be unfamiliar territory to many working in library and information services, but there are many techniques and tools available to help social scientists (into which category information professionals fall) analyse qualitative social media data. In his very accessible blog post, Wasim Ahmed suggests that a simple application is that of text analytics, which can include using sentiment analysis, to place bulk social media posts into categories of a particular topic, such as positive, negative or neutral. He goes on to say that other methods, such as social network analysis, can help to analyse online communities and the relationships between them (Ahmed, 2017).

Being able to group or code library users' thoughts, perceptions and opinions with regard to sentiment can start to provide real insight into what they want from their library and information services. Such market research data can then hugely complement data that might have been obtained from other more traditional methods, such as surveys or focus groups. In that case the market research intelligence is validated, but in other cases you might get insight from user communities that have been more difficult to engage with previously. Or users who have engaged with social media may have different requirements and expectations, and by using text analytics and data analysis you have been made aware of this.

There are many online platforms and applications available which enable big data analysis of social media. However, for the novice librarian, trying their hand at data science, qualitative methods such as thematic analysis, which is simply 'a method for identifying, analysing and reporting patterns within data' (Braun and Clarke, 2006, 79), can be an effective way to gain insights and collect data. It could be as simple as taking a selection of tweets or comments and manually highlighting the themes that come out within them. Alternatively, to keep things simple you might just copy and paste all your text into a Microsoft Word document and search for particular strings of characters in order to identify trends or sentiments. Similarly generating word clouds from social media text could allow you to visualise your data.

Even performing this data analysis in a rudimentary way can bring deeper insight and deeper analysis of this data may provide you with market research intelligence. Ultimately the conversations, comments and general user activity in a library's social media environments can feed into the marketing cycle not just in providing insight, but also in continuing the dialogue with users throughout the different stages of the cycle.

User engagement data and dialogue (outcomes measurement and evaluation)

Potter suggests that good marketing involves a continuous dialogue with your users or customers (2012, xiv). Therefore, continuing with the marketing theme, it is appropriate to look at where social media can be used effectively with the other parts of the marketing cycle that I identified above, those of outcomes measurement and evaluation. I suggest that both activities involve some kind of dialogue and engagement, which could be realised through social media. There are several ways in which the impact of a particular marketing and publicity campaign can be measured. These include obtaining metrics on how many times a web page has been viewed or trying to ascertain how a library user heard of a particular service or resource. In many cases data can be used and analysed in order to measure the impact and outcomes of a particular campaign. For example, if the outcome of a campaign was to increase the number of library users or visits from a particular demographic then user registration data or headcount data might be used to demonstrate this. Similarly, if the intended outcome of a campaign was to increase the usage of a specific e-resource, then usage statistics could be used in order to evidence the achievement (or not) of the outcomes. These would be quantitative measures, but they could easily be complemented by some qualitative data obtained through social media channels.

Data mining

Data mining is the practice of uncovering patterns and other valuable information from large data. If you were to do some data mining around given search terms across your social media channels (e.g. associated with your campaign and in social media posts which mention your library) then you may well realise a whole dataset that had previously gone unnoticed. Performing similar sentiment analysis or text analytics as identified in the market research phase would allow the surfacing of any qualitative data generated through social media that could validate the outcomes measurement and indeed the evaluation of a piece of library marketing. For example, as well as being able to statistically prove that your e-resources usage has increased, you may be able to back this up with data generated through comments and posts about your e-resources on your library Facebook site, or responses to your tweets in which you have publicised your particular e-resources. The data collection and analysis should be done in a timely fashion in line with the publicity campaign.

Service improvements and customer services

The use of social media for generating dialogue with library users doesn't need to be exclusive to your marketing activity. Indeed, speaking and listening to their users is something that library and information services need to do all the time, not just for marketing but also for service evaluation and quality assurance. Library user surveys, focus groups, UX methods, suggestions, comments and complaints forms are all commonly used methods for engaging with library users. Such methods might be regarded as 'traditional' in that they are very visible and tangible. Even if your library user survey is being carried out online, or you use an online suggestion form, these engagement activities are deliberate in that they are intended to be part of a dialogue and so form part of your service evaluation cycle. All of these methods are well used in library and information services across all sectors, and each can generate rich quantitative and qualitative data which is then used to evaluate service delivery and inform service developments.

Imagine if you were then able to supplement this data with what people are saying about your service when you haven't formally asked them through a survey or a comments card. Imagine if you could simply hear what your users are saying while they chat in the café or in their reading group discussions. Social media can partly achieve this and add further to what is already a potentially very rich data set. People often say they visit social media to 'be in the same place as their customers' or to 'hear what people are saying about [a given topic]'. You can do this with social media. However, there is no point in simply 'being in the same space as your users' unless you are going to engage with them and act on the conversation that you have. Engagement might occur through publicising your services, resources and events on social media, or through your strategic approach to timed tweets and posts. The dialogue happens when you engage with the responses to such activity or even just by 'listening in' to what users might be saying on social media. It might be that a particular Facebook post about an event has generated some conversation between library users about other events that they might like to see in your library. It is this type of dialogue, which you hadn't even asked for, that could very well prove to be important intelligence about your users' requirements and expectations. Once you are aware of this

136   DATA-DRIVEN DECISIONS

you might want to apply data mining and data analysis techniques to all of your social media channels. Again, you might consider analysing such data sources by particular sentiments or character strings in order to focus on specific themes or issues.

Altmetrics

I could not really discuss social media and libraries without at least a mention of altmetrics. In some ways it might have been appropriate to commence the chapter by introducing the fact that working with social media metrics and data is nothing new to library and information professionals in that they have been championing and taking responsibility for bibliometrics and more recently altmetrics for quite some time. However, altmetrics which makes use of social media data is not actually concerned with decision making (at least not by library and information professionals) which is my justification for leaving it until this point in the chapter.

But what is altmetrics? Priem has a useful and simple definition: 'altmetrics (short for "alternative metrics") [is] an approach to uncovering previously invisible traces of scholarly impact by observing activity in online tools and systems' (Priem, 2014, 263).

Altmetrics has emerged from traditional bibliometrics as the sources of metrical data about research and scholarship have expanded to include the web and social media. Showers (2016) suggests that the current abundance of all metrics around research and scholarship can be traced back to libraries' original interest in being able to demonstrate the impact of research and scholarship (e.g. through journal impact factor). Nowadays altmetrics have become increasingly popular as a means of scholars and institutions measuring the impact of their work, alongside bibliometric techniques. Libraries (mainly research and academic libraries) are at the centre of the development of altmetrics, as indeed they were at the centre of developing bibliometrics, in that librarians play a role in helping to support scholars and researchers in their understanding and measuring their impact (Showers, 2016, 62).

The relevance of altmetrics to this chapter lies in the 'alternative' sources that altmetrics makes use of – what we are referring to as 'social media'. In his book *Altmetrics*, Andy Tattersall goes into some detail as to how altmetrics work and what the role of the librarian is in the collection and analysis of altmetrics. He lists many sources of alternative metrics and categorises them into social networks (e.g. Facebook, Google+, LabRoots, LinkedIn, Mendeley, ResearchGate, Twitter), collaborative platforms (e.g. Google Docs, Hivebench), audio and video channels (e.g. Audioboom, Explain Everything, Mixcloud,

USING DIGITAL AND SOCIAL MEDIA TO INFORM MANAGEMENT DECISIONS 137

Vimeo, YouTube), infographic and visualisation platforms (e.g. F1000Posters, figshare, Impactstory, SlideShare) and blogging and informal methods of communication (Tattersall, 2016). The point is not to simply list the vast (and ever increasing) amount of altmetric sources available but to see it in the context of the work of the library and information professional, as they need not only to be aware of these sources, but also to know how to collect and analyse altmetric data for the purposes of scholarly communications. This is aided in part by Altmetric.com, an organisation whose primary function is to focus on article level altmetrics in order to support the library and research communities in demonstrating the impact of research (Adie, 2016). It does this by providing up-to-date information from a wide range of social media, including many of those listed above. Altmetric.com fully monitors 17 platforms in total including reference management tools such as Mendeley and many other sources including Wikipedia, LinkedIn, Facebook, Google+, Twitter and YouTube. Altmetric.com focus on the qualitative analysis of the web and social media platforms, applying text analysis and sentiment analysis to their data in order to better understand what people are saying about research and how they feel about it.

Such work uses data-driven approaches, and academic library departments have been quick to develop scholarly communications and research support teams whose role it is to manage and interpret this altmetric data alongside the bibliometric data that they had traditionally taken responsibility for. Although altmetric data might not necessarily inform library-oriented decisions, knowledge and understanding of how the data is generated and what it means, particularly qualitative altmetric data, are essential competencies for library and information professionals. This now includes knowledge and skills in some of the data science techniques of textual analysis and sentiment analysis as discussed above. For those involved in scholarly communications and research support, being able to analyse altmetric data in order to support the research activity of their institution is a key emerging skillset, and one that is transferable to analysing the library's own alternative digital data sources.

Web-based analytics

While the main focus of this chapter has really been about qualitative data sources drawn from social media, plenty of quantitative data can also be generated from web and digital sources. Therefore, to bring the chapter to a close it is appropriate to discuss briefly potential web-based library analytics. Analytics have become increasingly commonplace within the library and

138   DATA-DRIVEN DECISIONS

information service environment. Showers suggests that libraries, along with archives, museums and galleries, find themselves ideally placed to exploit the full potential of analytics, as 'they have long been familiar with the potential of statistics and data for informing everything from service development to measurement of impact and value' (Showers, 2015, xxv).

Analytics refers to the discovery and communication of what data actually means. In a library sense it is about using the analysis of library-generated data to tell a story, or provide evidence of something, both of which can lead to decision making. A good example of an analytics service is Google Analytics, which provides an analysis of website data, including the number of people who visit a website, where they are located and how they have accessed the website. Libraries have lots of data available to them, including website data, but also things like usage statistics, gate counts, headcounts. Much of this can be analysed at different levels, such as by user type or demographic. The resultant analysis would therefore be regarded as analytics and how such data informs decisions has very much been the focus of this book, so we now look at a framework developed some years ago in order to measure the web impact (data about website and social media usage) of cultural heritage institutions, a category into which many library and information services fall. The framework uses a variety of web metrics and is presented as a case study example of public sector institutions making the most of the web-based and social media metrics that they have at their disposal in order to inform decision making and service development (Stuart, 2015). The framework depicted in Table 12.1 uses four main categories: data collected internally (e.g. by the institution itself), data collected externally (e.g. by a social media platform), user behaviour (evidence of web activity) and user traces (evidence of engagement with web platforms and social media).

Table 12.1 *Framework that measures web impact through internal and external data on user behaviour and user traces*

	User behaviour	User traces
Internal	Page views Hits	Comments Feedback Contributions
External	Google searches Traffic rank Social media views	Web mentions In links and URL citations Facebook likes Social network friends

Web analytics of user behaviour are effectively the number of visits to a website or a particular page. Google Analytics is a commonly used tool for measuring web page user behaviour, and such tools can be used to track when, where and how a particular website or web page was accessed. For example, detailed analytics could provide metrics telling you when a particular web page was visited by someone using a particular type of device from a specific location. As well as providing a picture of where users are located and how and when they are accessing your site, such metrics can also inform decision making. For example, you might want to analyse whether a page is getting a particular amount of traffic from a particular demographic. Is it because the content is extremely useful, or perhaps because users cannot find their way through the web pages? Either way such analysis could inform your decisions about web page development. Such analytics are usually kept internally to the organisation, but external user behaviour analytics can also be used in order to analyse your web impact. This might involve using an externally provided global web traffic service which will provide comparisons of web traffic between different organisations or different types of organisation. This could effectively provide you with data about how your library's website is performing as compared to another 'competitor' organisation, which would be very valuable in a market research context. Other external user behaviour analytics would include services such as Google Trends which provide metrics and data about what subjects and topics people are searching for rather than which particular websites they are searching.

Social media views can also be used as external user behaviour metrics, but they effectively only provide you with usage data. However, user traces can provide more detailed analytics on how users are engaging and such activity resonates with the application of altmetrics, as discussed above. Users' comments on library blog platforms would be an example of such engagement, while social media metrics (external) can provide rich data on your overall web impact, including metrics about 'likes', 'shares', 'follows' and 'retweets', but the analysis of these as metrics requires some understanding of social network analysis. Most social media platforms have their own analytics tools, which you can use (although you may need to invest some time in learning how to use them effectively). Similarly, there are many other tools available for analysing metrics and generating big data across multiple social media platforms (e.g. Sendible, Semrush, Awario).

Ultimately, using a web impact framework allows you to join up your users' digital behaviours and digital traces, providing a fuller picture of how they are engaging (or not) with your library's digital presence.

Summary

In this chapter we've explored some key examples of how digital and social media platforms can provide alternative sources of data to library and information services, in order that service-level decisions can be made and validated.

The analysis techniques and approaches discussed in this chapter are associated with the data science discipline. However, as library and information roles emerge and develop in the 21st century, there is a clear need for library and information professionals to become more proficient in data-oriented work. The introductory techniques and topics discussed during this chapter are a simple way to start on this journey and I hope offers a springboard for more exploration of less obvious routes to your data-driven decisions.

13 Starting from Scratch: Building a Data Culture at the University of Westminster

Sarah Maule

Background

The University of Westminster (UoW) was the first polytechnic university in London, and opened in 1839. The University has a rich history, and supports a variety of subjects from the arts to business. Based in central London, the University is spread over numerous buildings in the West End, Marylebone and Harrow in West London. It currently has four site libraries spread across its different locations, each of which has its own subject focus, style and quirks.

When in 2013 the UK government announced it would lift the cap on the number of students individual universities could accept, the UoW, like many institutions, faced significant financial pressures as student numbers inevitably reduced. From 2015 the cap was removed entirely, and to respond the management had to make some significant cuts to remain financially viable. For UoW this included a large-scale redundancy exercise and restructuring, which included the library and archive services.

As there are four site libraries, students benefit from the flexibility of choosing where to study and what environment they want to study in. Each library site at Westminster feels unique and differs from each other in its environment. However, while refurbishments and investment had been carried out in some library sites, others needed real attention. Although students can choose where they study, books and resources for courses are at specific sites, often close to where students on those courses have their lectures, so often students would spend most of their time at their 'home' site. The inconsistency in investment and refurbishments alongside students having home sites made library users' experiences incomparable.

Before the restructure the Library and Archives Service had a single senior manager for library sites and enquiry points, and one senior manager for academic liaison and collection development. There were cuts and reduction in staffing in many aspects of the service, along with significant changes to the senior management team, so frontline senior managers (site library services managers) took on much more responsibility and ability to develop services. Arguably the service had been somewhat stagnant for several years, and there was little room to review or suggest innovation. Senior management had avoided making changes to services, and it felt as if the service had fallen behind other library services at competitor institutions. Indeed, social media platforms were only recently introduced, LibGuides was just being established, and online library chat for users was relatively new and not widely promoted. The change in management approach and the restructure as a whole presented an opportunity for the senior management team to finally focus on reviewing and changing service delivery.

The data we had

Each library site had a site library services manager who had detailed knowledge of the physical site and enquiry points. However, this knowledge was mostly anecdotal, with no data to back up suspicions and feelings. The quantitative data which was available was not regularly analysed, discussed or used to inform decision making. More importance was placed on the available qualitative data, but it was limited and not analysed as part of a regular planning cycle, nor did it form the basis for a cycle of improvements or progression of the service.

A driver for change

A new director of the Library and Archives Service started at the end of 2016 along with myself as one of the site library services managers. In order to react to further financial changes and constraints it was anticipated that senior managers may have to cut services or resources for users. In preparation for this I set out to analyse usage of the library sites and hoped to find where savings could be made. I had previously worked in a role where data was required for making significant decisions in changes of service and assumed the same would be required at UoW. However, I quickly realised there was no comparable culture or ethos, and I set about changing this in order to further professionalise the service and back up decisions with data.

Overnight opening case study

During the summer of 2017 the site library services managers were given the costings for delivering overnight opening of the four library sites for the first time. This was the largest portion of spend of the operations budget and had increased year on year, as demand for extra opening came in sporadically from different academic departments and courses.

Table 13.1 depicts the opening hours at UoW for two semesters in 2017 at the four sites.

Table 13.1 *The original evening opening hours at the four sites of the UoW, semesters 1 and 2, academic year 2017/18*

	LW1	LW2	LW3	LW4	LW5	LW6	LW7	LW8	LW9	LW10	LW11	LW12	VW1	VW2	VW3	Exam 1	Exam 2
									Semester 1								
Marylebone			11pm						24/7				11pm	Varied		24/7	
Harrow			11pm						24/7				11pm	Closed		24/7	
Cavendish			11pm						24/7				11pm	Closed		24/7	
Regent			11pm						24/7				11pm	Closed		24/7	
	LW1	LW2	LW3	LW4	LW5	LW6	LW7	LW8	LW9	LW10	LW11	LW12	VW1	VW2	?	Exam 1	Exam 2
									Semester 2								
Marylebone									24/7								
Harrow					11pm								24/7				
Cavendish					11pm								24/7				
Regent					11pm								24/7				

The costings for overnight opening were made available too late to change anything for the upcoming academic year, largely because there was no time to consult key stakeholders on any drastic changes. However, knowing that the overnight opening hours model was difficult to communicate and regularly received negative student feedback, I began work to investigate usage data and understand this service better, the user needs, and where we could improve.

Journey

As outlined in the toolkit my colleagues and I started by ascertaining our data need, asking:

> 'Is the current overnight opening model cost effective and is it suiting users' needs during term time?'

To answer this we needed to investigate the following data queries:

- How and when students were using overnight opening?
- Which library site was the busiest and which was the quietest?

Answering these questions would help inform our decisions on cost effectiveness and shape any changes to the model, instead of relying on our

144   DATA-DRIVEN DECISIONS

assumptions. From our own knowledge and experience of running frontline library services we felt that:

- Overnight opening should change and not be offered seven days a week but scaled back to five days a week maximum.
- Overnight opening should be extended to cover all library sites during the second term, and not just limited to the seemingly busiest site, Marylebone.

It was clear we needed evidence to prove or dispel these theories, and data would play a vital role.

To begin I started looking at the data and data sources currently available, then put them into categories (Table 13.2).

Table 13.2 *Data types and data gained from various sources for this case study*

Data type	Data gained	Source
Quantitative	Student numbers at each site	Student Record System (SRS Web)
Quantitative	Capacity of each site used	SCONUL return
Quantitative	Hourly overnight headcounts	Spreadsheet log completed by security staff
Qualitative	Student feedback	National Student Survey (NSS) free text comments Feedback cards Focus groups Student representative forum minutes Complaints

The spreadsheet log showing hourly headcounts was compiled by security officers who oversee and supervise overnight opening. This data began in 2012 and while it was collected manually, which allowed for user error, it was beneficial for several reasons. The data was accessible, covered a substantial timeframe, offered the ability to investigate trends, and didn't require gathering further data. It had been collected daily, during the security officers' hourly patrols. As the data had been collected in such a granular way, I could not just examine how many students set out to use the library overnight, I could also find out how long students would stay for within the space. This was a rich and exhaustive data source which I was very grateful for, especially considering how little importance had been placed on data within the service

BUILDING A DATA CULTURE AT THE UNIVERSITY OF WESTMINSTER   145

previously. This was proven by the fact that this comprehensive data source had been collected for over five years, but had never been interrogated or analysed before.

However, the data wasn't perfect and ready to go. It was currently being input into a template that could not be easily analysed or used, as depicted in Table 13.3.

Table 13.3   *Hourly headcounts at Harrow Library, 23 September to 8 October 2013; an example of a poorly laid out spreadsheet*

	A	B	C	D	E	F	G	H	I	J	K
1	Harrow Library 24/7 hourly headcounts 2013-14										
2			Date	5pm	6pm	7pm	8pm	9pm	10pm	11pm	12am
3											
4	Learning	Mon	23/09/2013				16	13	14	6	
5	Week 1	Tue	24/09/2013				23	24	13	3	
6		Wed	25/09/2013				38	31	19	3	
7		Thu	26/09/2013				18	13	12	6	
8		Fri	27/09/2013	36	44	18	19	14	9	9	
9		Sat	28/09/2013	32	19	17	16	18	9	4	
10		Sun	29/09/2013	52	42	29	17	13	8	5	
11	Learning	Mon	30/09/2013				43	34	24	15	
12	Week 2	Tue	01/10/2013				34	23	24	6	
13		Wed	02/10/2013				25	31	18	19	
14		Thu	03/10/2013				32	26	13	5	
15		Fri	04/10/2013	65	52	34	23	20	16	4	
16		Sat	05/10/2013	23	21	16	6	12	13	4	
17		Sun	06/10/2013	36	30	34	28	20	7	4	
18	Learning	Mon	07/10/2013				34	38	26	20	
19	Week 3	Tue	08/10/2013				47	52	36	34	

Autumn term 2013   Spring term 2014   Summer term 2014   2013-14 in total   30 & 31 December 2013

As you can see, it was presented in an odd format; lots of empty rows and columns, spread across multiple tabs and documents. This did not allow for any analysis, let alone a quick pivot table. Any headcounts with numbers under ten were identified as low usage, however there was no cross reference to the capacity of the library and there had never been any discussions over what was considered low usage.

Inputting this data took up staff time, and again was a manual process. One dedicated staff member on each library site had to collect the physically printed logbook and manually input the numbers into Excel files. These files were broken down by academic year, then site, and stored on the staff shared drive.

On reflection, the current practice of data collection was perhaps the main reason why no investigative work had been carried out into how students were using the overnight service, and no analysis into what changes could be made. The data was incomprehensive and did not provide the full picture easily. The fact that the data was scattered among different tabs and documents was off-putting and ultimately made it very time consuming to collate the data and get it into a usable state.

146 DATA-DRIVEN DECISIONS

Getting started with quantitative data

We spent time amalgamating all legacy spreadsheets into one cloud-based master document, with clear headings and the ability to interrogate data quickly. It was unfortunate but necessary, and again shows how important it is to set up your data in a format that can be analysed in the future.

Mapping the data was made possible by categorising the headcount data into learning weeks and terms. Overnight opening would start on a different date each academic year, however it was always the start of learning week six of the autumn term. These categories were added as headings; this way weekly trends could be investigated and the data was fully comparable. Finally, after a long and tedious process the data was easy to find, analyse and understand, as seen in Table 13.4.

Table 13.4 *Hourly headcounts at Cavendish Library, two weeks of autumn term 2014/15; an example of a well laid out spreadsheet*

Year	Term	Site	Learning week	Day	8pm	9pm	10pm	11pm	12am	1am	2am
2014/15	Autumn	Cavendish	6	Mon	54	29	25	22	20	18	16
2014/15	Autumn	Cavendish	6	Tue	62	52	40	31	20	15	10
2014/15	Autumn	Cavendish	6	Wed	45	37	20	22	19	20	19
2014/15	Autumn	Cavendish	6	Thu	34	29	19	10	10	10	9
2014/15	Autumn	Cavendish	6	Fri	18	13	12	9	9	10	10
2014/15	Autumn	Cavendish	6	Sat	18	17	7	10	7	7	4
2014/15	Autumn	Cavendish	6	Sun	59	52	27	25	21	15	15
2014/15	Autumn	Cavendish	7	Mon	68	50	39	27	21	16	11
2014/15	Autumn	Cavendish	7	Tue	49	32	24	20	18	14	12
2014/15	Autumn	Cavendish	7	Wed	47	33	34	32	27	25	24
2014/15	Autumn	Cavendish	7	Thu	55	34	25	14	14	5	7
2014/15	Autumn	Cavendish	7	Fri	40	35	22	31	9	6	6
2014/15	Autumn	Cavendish	7	Sat	49	42	39	15	10	4	2
2014/15	Autumn	Cavendish	7	Sun	71	74	68	65	31	19	13
2014/15	Autumn	Cavendish	8	Mon	63	50	39	29	20	15	17

Getting started with qualitative data

Moving on to the qualitative data available brought a nice change of pace after dealing with so many numbers. The National Student Survey (NSS) provides a rich source of data as thousands of students complete it every year, across all campuses and disciplines. I had the previous year's NSS comments available and feedback cards handed in at enquiry points but felt there was no need to gather older NSS comments from students who had graduated more than two years ago. It was my intention to find out how I could meet current users' needs better. Having a snapshot of the most recent students' thoughts was already outdated but by no more than nine months.

I created codes for the NSS comments in order to draw out feedback on library opening hours, ignoring and not coding any that did not mention the library, and coded those that mentioned the library by the seemingly major areas the author felt passionate about (academic study support, library space, opening hours or resources). Then I sorted each coded comment by colour and circulated the data to colleagues responsible for each area, in case they would find it useful to analyse in the future.

A significant majority of the NSS comments and feedback cards were complaints about the current overnight opening model not meeting their needs in Term 2 (the spring term). This data further confirmed the site library services managers' feelings that the overnight opening model should be expanded to cover all library sites. The qualitative data backed up and supported that outcome.

Compiling the data

Compiling all the data, qualitative and quantitative, took more time than I first envisaged and was a learning curve for future projects. I couldn't start analysis as quickly as I would have liked, however not rushing the data compiling was beneficial in the long run. Indeed, I didn't have to go back and search for additional data, as the data gathering and compiling stage had been so thorough.

Fortunately, analysing the data was a quick task. I was quickly able to ascertain our busiest site, once capacity of each site was cross-referenced, and that led to many other results which were not part of the original scope but were helpful to see and discuss. Trends and patterns between sites, likely due to the differences of the disciplines taught at each site, started to emerge. However, as the aim was to produce an overnight opening model which was more consistent than the current one, these trends and patterns were unlikely to change the proposed model. It was beneficial to be able to observe trends and patterns between sites, which ultimately gave library managers deeper understanding of overnight opening and how the service was actually used.

Analysis

Now the time had come to investigate the data, I could see if any previous assumptions were correct, and what the data could tell me. I disregarded any data from vacation weeks as these times do not give a true representation of user needs during term time, as per the data query. Overnight opening is not offered during vacation, however there are headcounts until the 11 p.m. closing time. These numbers could easily have skewed the headcounts for 6–11 p.m. during learning weeks and overnight opening and were therefore excluded.

148 DATA-DRIVEN DECISIONS

Patterns

One of the first patterns to emerge was the noticeable drop in overnight usage on Friday and Saturday evenings, which was on average 40% quieter than the busiest overnight usage evening, Wednesday. This was significant and confirmed a suspicion we had that weekends were quieter, but we didn't have any evidence of this until now. As the data had been gathered over more than five years it was clear to see this trend was established and therefore was not specific to the most recent academic year (shown in Figure 13.1).

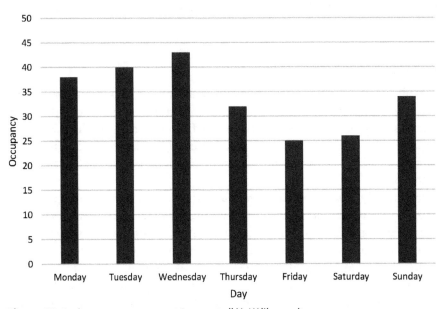

Figure 13.1 *Average occupancy at 1 a.m. at all UoW library sites*

Another pattern I identified was the usage of each of the four libraries during overnight opening. It was shockingly low at one of our sites, with only 4% of the library in use at the 1 a.m. headcount (Figure 13.2 opposite).

This called into question value for money, something we as library managers had considered but not placed great emphasis on until this point. The most used library had on average only 12% of the library capacity in use at the 1 a.m. headcount. Therefore, even the most popular library was not being used extensively. I will discuss this in more depth in the presentation to the Student Union representatives below.

We used mostly bar graphs and a few pie charts as visualisations. The bar graphs made comparisons between sites easy for those looking at the data. They were clearly labelled, in bold colours identified for each site or year

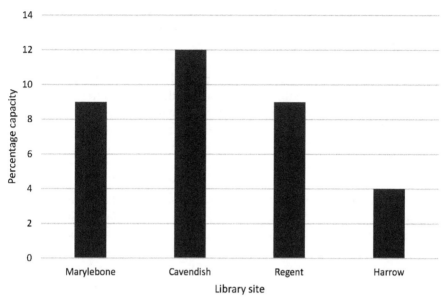

Figure 13.2 *Percentage capacity at different UoW library sites at 1 a.m.*

being compared, and we applied data labels. We used filters to break the data down so graphs weren't unwieldly or hard to interpret, and dealt with one area specifically, for example, usage by days of the week, or usage by learning week. After producing the graphs I needed for my presentation, I asked a colleague to look with a fresh pair of eyes and tell me if there were any follow-up queries they felt they raised. This was a good way to see if the data and presentation matched the findings I was trying to convey to an audience.

I included the data visualisations and my conclusions in a presentation to key stakeholders. This included a new draft model for overnight opening, which clearly identified the differences between what was currently on offer and the proposed changes based on the data findings. Changing opening hours can be a delicate situation for library users and I was keen to ensure that the reasoning for changing the model was clearly explained and had support from stakeholders.

Conclusions and action

It was clear that the overnight library opening was underused and that the inconsistency in overnight opening across sites was negatively impacting student experience. Yet from the first day of term many students ask about 24/7 library opening and when it begins. Prospective students are even known

150   DATA-DRIVEN DECISIONS

to ask about it on open days. It can be argued that staying up all night studying in the library with classmates is seen as a rite of passage within university, and one students are keen to try.

The data was showing overnight opening was only popular on Sunday–Thursday nights, and we knew from all of the data together that we needed to change our opening hours to reflect this usage pattern. However, changing our existing hours, and to be seen to be taking opening hours away from users, could have been problematic. It could ultimately lead to complaints and student dissatisfaction. Knowing this I consulted my fellow members of the senior management team and we discussed the approach that would hopefully be the path of least resistance. We agreed that the importance of strong communication, as early as possible, was the best approach to take. Communications with all library staff had been few and far between before the recent change in senior management, and I took this as an opportunity to communicate these changes with all staff at whatever level and encourage them to advocate, spread the word about these changes, and discuss them with their contacts outside the library department at the earliest opportunity.

In February 2018 I gave a presentation to the library senior management team and operational managers, showing my findings and asked for feedback. Afterwards I made a few tweaks to the presentation and met the current Student Union president and vice-presidents. This was extremely insightful. They had detailed knowledge of the student body, students' working patterns and experience of studying and fully supported us in our proposal to change the overnight opening hours. They explained that a large proportion of students with part-time jobs are in the hospitality sector and therefore work Friday and/or Saturday nights. They knew that many students procrastinated over the weekends until they felt the pressure of upcoming deadlines, and this was why Sunday night overnight opening was more popular than some weekday overnight openings. This was further evidence that the proposed model would fit with students' needs.

The final part of the face-to-face consultation then took place. I met registry managers, who are responsible for frontline services to students regarding their course of study and assessments. I presented them with the findings, now with the additional context gained from meeting the Student Union representatives and explained that they supported our proposals. The registry managers felt the change in hours would function operationally and would not lead to claims from students saying they were unable to complete their coursework because the library was closed on Friday and Saturday nights. They also felt there was another reason to reduce overnight library opening hours to five nights a week instead of seven. Although we thought it unlikely that any students stayed overnight in the library seven days per week, in not providing a space for library study every night of the week we were indirectly encouraging students to take a break from non-stop studying.

The library senior management team felt that if the presentations to the Student Union and registry managers throughout February–April went well, then a short paper noting the changes should be circulated to members of the Student Experience Committee, who were due to meet in April 2018. The Student Experience Committee is made up of professional services directors across the university and elected members of the Student Union, including the president and vice-presidents. Their focus is to 'promote student engagement and sense of community and to review, monitor and enhance student satisfaction and all aspects of the student experience' (UoW, 2021). This paper would be read by other stakeholders who might not have been present in the presentation stage, such as staff from Estates and Security. It was also another opportunity to circulate the data and explain why we had decided to change the library's opening hours before any changes in October 2018.

We wrote a short paper of around 400 words for the committee, summarising the changes and including the data in an appendix, should anyone want to investigate how we had interpreted it. My experience of writing papers for committees is that the shorter they are the better, especially if you are not presenting them verbally. My paper was noted with no need for it to be approved – the committee was happy for the changes to be made by the library service.

This now set in motion the final stages of the project, when we focused mainly on communications and marketing. There was a substantial period before the changes came into effect, six months, so no part of the communications were rushed or took library users by surprise. Library managers attended the next scheduled Student Forum meetings to take place to explain the new overnight model, which would come into effect the next academic year. Course representatives notified the change to students before the summer break and were able to respond to any questions they had.

We updated frontline library staff of the future changes in regular communications to all staff and team meetings throughout the process. I circulated a recording I had made of my presentation to the Student Experience Committee to all library staff to watch and take in. Staff had an opportunity to provide feedback on the new model, which we analysed for potential risks.

These were some of the comments we received from library staff:

152   DATA-DRIVEN DECISIONS

I think that is a really good compromise. It should prevent students from 'camping out' in the Library from Friday evening through to Monday morning, which is something that a small minority of our students do during 24/7 opening periods, and which is incredibly unhealthy for them. They can hardly keep their eyes open on Monday, and yet go straight from 'hand-in time' at 10 a.m. to further lectures and seminars that same day.

Opening hours should regularly be reviewed.

A clearer and more consistent structure for the opening times.

Embedding the new model

Staff supported the new model, which was encouraging. It was positive to see feedback encouraging regular reviews of an area of service, which is something I hadn't heard from colleagues before this exercise. Liaison staff were urged to disseminate the new model with their academic contacts before the summer break so there was a lengthy notice period for stakeholders to understand the change. This was all to minimise negative reactions to the change as much as possible at the start of the autumn term.

From late September onwards we rolled out marketing and promotion of the new overnight opening hours. The internal marketing team had created some eye-catching marketing material and cleverly tied in a message about the online resources that are available overnight, including our live chat service. This was a subtle way to remind library users that the service is not limited to physical space and when the library is closed support and resources are available.

We reminded staff about the new model in a start of term briefing before the beginning of the new academic year. This ensured the message going out to library users was clear and consistent. This was the first time that opening hours were uniform across all sites and it was positive to see that students did not seem confused when they enquired about them. This was simply not the case before the review.

Lessons learned and reflection

Although this project was on the simpler side of using data to make a decision, the results were far-reaching. As the findings were presented with the decision on the service change, it was the first example of the Customer Services Department using data to review and change the service. This was

BUILDING A DATA CULTURE AT THE UNIVERSITY OF WESTMINSTER 153

the beginning of a culture change where gathering, analysing and using data was encouraged and at the heart of decision making. Creating a data culture takes time, however this project showed that the time spent was worthwhile.

This project was a catalyst within the Library and Archives Service. As I previously mentioned, senior staffing had just changed when this project was started. It was an interim structure and when these changes to overnight opening went live UoW welcomed the first new external head of the Library and Archives Service as a permanent position for over a decade. This new post holder was a keen advocate in gathering and analysing data. They started the role with similar feelings to mine, shocked at the lack of data gathered throughout the service, and set the expectation of more data collection from the outset of their appointment.

Once the changes to the overnight opening started and students responded positively to the new model, frontline staff in particular felt confident that collecting data was not a pointless task and has multiple benefits. Receiving fewer complaints at the enquiry points in Term 2 inspired some staff members to suggest other types of data we could gather to gain increased insight into the service. Overall the project was extremely satisfying. Making a significant change to a previously stagnant service was daunting, but it delivered multiple benefits for staff and students. Taking steps to change the culture and ethos of data collection within the department was always going to take time, however this project was the spark needed to stimulate colleagues to come around to a new way of working.

We now had evidence to prioritise making data collection automatic and less manual within the department. This would make future projects involving data collection less time consuming and more routine.

14 Back to the Drawing Board: How Data Visualisation Techniques Informed Service Delivery during the COVID-19 Pandemic

Elaine Sykes

Setting the scene

Liverpool John Moores University (LJMU) is a vibrant institution in a thriving city. It was created in 1992 from Liverpool Polytechnic and built on the foundations of various educational establishments dating back to 1823. It has a real heart for supporting its students, many of whom come from non-traditional backgrounds.

I have worked at LJMU for 14 years, over 10 of which in the Library Services. My current role is Team Leader for the Business Administration Team, which covers lots of different things – data is certainly a large part, but definitely not all I do. I also have responsibility for monitoring finance, administration, health and safety, compliance with General Data Protection Regulations (GDPR) and anything else that comes along! In an organisation like ours, we need to be able to turn our hands to most things as we only have a small team of staff compared with some other institutions. This actually has pros and cons – although we don't always have the staff capacity to deliver everything we'd like to, we have lots of opportunities to gain new experiences and develop new skills, and our management are always very supportive of staff who want to try new initiatives.

As a result, I've been actively encouraged to develop my own skills and experience with respect to data analysis. I have a maths background, but most of what I know about using data I've learned on the job and picked up as I've gone along. I now co-ordinate most data analyses for Library Services, the importance of which has greatly increased in the last few years as they are used to inform senior managers for operational and strategic decisions.

One of the biggest successes that we've had in getting more understanding and richer insights from our data has been in employing data visualisation. This case study will outline this journey, the highs and lows and why we believe it is such a valuable approach, especially during the pandemic.

Background

Over the last ten years in the post, I have spent a lot of time improving our data collections and analysis methods. My initial developments concentrated on our data collection methods and really getting to understand our data, its strength and limitations. One of my biggest challenges in starting our data journey was getting people to be able to relate any findings back to their real-world experiences or to interpret the results in the appropriate context. I've found that people don't often question results if they're given in the form of numbers or a graph, but sometimes when you relate findings back to real-world situations they don't make sense. As an example, when I started in my current role, on my first viewing of our gate count data we occasionally had negative entries. Now, if that were true then some major disaster would have befallen the library! Some closer inspection proved that some of the formulas had gone awry, but because no one had related this back to the real world, no one had ever questioned it.

Although improving our data collection and formatting is an ongoing challenge and we still have several improvements to make, more recently our attention has turned to producing better analyses. By 'better' I really mean two things:

- deriving the richest insight from our data
- engaging our audience more with our analyses.

Both these aspirations have been greatly improved by embracing data visualisation techniques and tools to analyse and communicate our data. Previously, we were wedded to the Microsoft Office approach of Word documents with Excel graphs added in. They contained decent enough insights but weren't exactly gripping, so we started to explore other options.

Piktochart

Our first experiments into the foray of better data visualisation concerned using an online product called Piktochart. This is a specific infographic creation tool, perfect for creating visually engaging reports and analyses.

We used the new format to reconsider the content of our reports. Rather than including every possible visualisation, we only concentrated on including graphs and charts that delivered actionable insight to the end-users (library managers and faculty colleagues). We also considered whether there were any other ways that we could analyse data that would lead to richer insights. As a result, we included a scatter plot of library satisfaction against overall satisfaction (Figure 14.1). In the figure we split courses into courses which were deemed 'celebrate' and 'investigate' based on overall performance, and compared results for NSS Q19 (library resources) and Q27 (overall course satisfaction). In the graph we can see where courses did not correlate exactly across overall satisfaction and library satisfaction. This visualisation helped unearth some additional courses where we needed to pay attention – although their library score was high, it was lower than their overall score, showing that students were unhappy with some aspects of library provision.

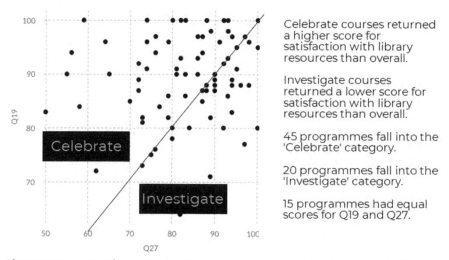

Figure 14.1 *Excerpt from a Faculty NSS report (using sample data) showing levels of satisfaction with library services divided into 'investigate' and 'celebrate' categories*

These new reports were a resounding success. Although they used the same data as we had displayed previously on Word and Excel documents, the difference in the audience engagement was remarkable, thanks to the new format and analyses. Suddenly, these reports were being shared with stakeholders outside the libraries and were being used to start discussions with faculty colleagues or to show to senior managers to help make the case for new initiatives such as additional investment.

Power BI

Before 2020, another tool we explored was Power BI. This is Microsoft's business intelligence platform, which allows you to create real-time, interactive analyses from several data sources.

I first encountered Power BI as a user, for a report on PC usage designed by our IT Department, in consultation with the Library. We were guided more by enthusiasm than skills in those early days and produced reports that looked visually impressive at first glance, but on closer inspection weren't all that useful, and at their worst actually left end-users feeling confused rather than delivering insight. This experience very much taught me that when it comes to designing dashboards, less is more!

One of the temptations when using this kind of software is to use it to produce every single type of visualisation as they look so impressive. However, unpack them a little and you often find that they don't really tell you all that much, or the same message could be conveyed more simply. This is one of the reasons why it is so important to identify your data needs at the start of the process, as once you start creating visualisations, it's so easy to get lost down various data rabbit holes. By establishing your data needs at the start (specifying what it is that you want to know) you can refer back to them and only select those visualisations which help address them.

One of the big challenges to using Power BI is the level of data literacy that it requires. Most of us are used to using spreadsheets to view and store our data, so we format them in order to look nice on the screen. However, if you intend to use data visualisation software, you must format your data in a different way, which may seem rather laborious and over the top. Indeed, if you are creating a spreadsheet that you want people to look at, you need to summarise as much as possible, however, if you want to use a spreadsheet to sit underneath a Power BI report then include as much detail as possible. You also need to use columns for everything!

This shouldn't put you off – one of the main lessons of working with data, as Amy highlights, is to use appropriate formatting. It's well worth exploring and if you are not 100% sure about how to approach this then ask around. Organisations often have data teams, even if not in the library, so see whether there's anyone you can tap into for experience. The advantage of using systems like this is that once they're set up, you can effectively leave them running, or at the very most just refresh the data within them. Start small and then you can build up from there.

One of the best things about using data visualisation software to display data is its facility for users to customise their dashboards for themselves. You can include filters, slicers and other customisation options. I find this invaluable: whereas previously I would have to produce five versions of the same report (one per faculty), I can now produce just one report, for which end-users can select their own parameters. This saves me a lot of duplicated effort.

The challenges and advantages referenced above apply to any data visualisation software, such as Tableau or LibInsight. For us at LJMU, though, the final advantage of Power BI is that it links with the rest of the Microsoft Office suite, including MS Teams.

Case study: the pandemic

In 2020, along came COVID-19. As with staff in all other libraries, suddenly all we knew and did was upended as we tried to navigate all the resultant challenges from the pandemic.

We reopened one library in the summer of 2020. Because of the new COVID regulations, we had to rearrange spaces so as to be socially distant and, given the reduced number of study spaces, we introduced new rules around bookings to try and ensure that as many students as possible would be able to access study space. Although we are fortunate at LJMU to have some very experienced staff, in such unprecedented times we were making decisions based on best guesses, and had no idea what demand would be or whether they were the best fit for this new environment. As a result, we needed good data analytics to be able to provide quick feedback on how well these new rules and arrangements were working.

Fortunately (from the data perspective at least), as users had to book their study spaces in advance via the university's system Resource Booker, we had access to good data about who was booking to come in to the libraries. We also had our normal data sources of gate counts, headcounts and so on to draw on.

We set about designing a new dashboard to capture the information. Power BI really came into its own because of its ability for users to customise their dashboards, its instant analyses and its easy to use and understand dashboards, all ideally suited to meet the needs of the situation. When building an appropriate dashboard we genuinely followed the steps laid out in chapters 3 to 5 of this book: identify, collect and map.

As per the Chapter 3 guidance, in order to build the new dashboard we first needed to specify our data need. In this case our data query was: 'Who is using the library and what are the most typical patterns of usage?'

The data

As mentioned above, when identifying suitable data sources, the Resource Booker data was our first port of call. Although this is an automated data source, we weren't able to link to it directly, but instead received weekly data extracts, which weren't directly suitable for the kinds of analyses that we wanted to carry out so they required reorganisation known as data cleaning. This varied from correcting inconsistent data (e.g. Aldham and Aldham Robarts were both listed under libraries when there should only be one entry) to having to separate columns that include date and time information.

Data from Resource Booker also requires us to combine a couple of different data sources in order to ascertain the faculty, school and level of each student who made a booking. Although our very helpful and kind planning team have set up a couple of tools to help us manage this, it involves more manual input than would be ideal. As we run these reports weekly, you can imagine the time this can take.

In order to combine the different data sources, we used a helpful VLOOKUP function in Excel to be able to cross-reference two data tables, using the student number. Figure 14.2 shows what this looked like and gives a brief explanation of each element of this function.

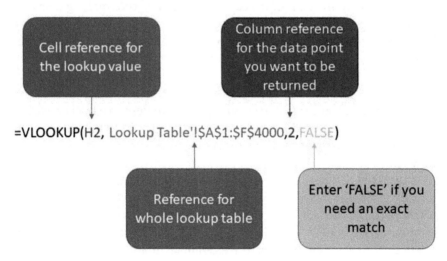

Figure 14.2 *The VLOOKUP function in Excel*

As Amy points out, being comfortable with spreadsheets and improving your skills in that area can only make your life easier when working with data so it's worth investing in. Manually cross-referencing two large data tables would be nearly impossible to do manually without using spreadsheets and formulas.

As we were working with personal data, and could identify which students were using the library, we needed to make sure to observe relevant legislation or privacy requirements such as GDPR, to ensure that we were processing data legally, securely and ethically.

Building the dashboard

Finally, once the data was in a suitable format, it was time to build the dashboard itself. This is where our data need and queries were so important. I actually wrote the data need out on a Post-it Note and had it next to my screen so I could keep it at the forefront of my mind.

Our data need naturally fell into two areas: who was using the library and what were the most typical patterns of usage. The next two sections outline our approach to each.

Analysing who uses the library

We wanted to better understand the characteristics of our users, from which schools or levels of study were using the libraries, as well as their demographic data such as gender and age.

We used the VLOOKUP function to cross-reference Resource Booker data with the student information system and get this information for each booking.

We were also interested in other demographic factors such as gender, age, POLAR (participation of local areas) quintile measures and declared disabilities. As much of this information would be classed as sensitive under GDPR legislation, we did not have access to this data at an individual level, but were able to run the student ID numbers through a bespoke tool which gave us this information as a summary. We compared the proportional breakdowns of these different demographic factors of library attendees with the overall university population, to see any over- or under-represented areas.

One such analysis led us to find that a high percentage of library users were in the 'widening access and participation' group. These are students who are in typically under-represented groups in higher education (e.g. first in family to attend university). This revelation helped evidence to our stakeholders the importance of our library space being open: although it wasn't always necessarily busy, for those who were using the library it was a lifeline.

162 DATA-DRIVEN DECISIONS

Analysing typical patterns of usage

Initial analyses on patterns of usage were as simple as counting the number of bookings per day for each library and ascertaining most common times of bookings. I later also included a measure to consider the number of bookings per student, to better understand whether we had fewer bookings from more students or fewer students making a lot of bookings.

We included headcount data, expressed as a percentage of overall capacity for each library, to better understand the busiest days or times. Again, this required some reformatting of the data in order to make it compatible with Power BI. As Amy suggested, longer term it would be better if this data were already stored in such a way that it could be linked to Power BI automatically, but that would be a larger project, requiring a redesign of our whole headcount collection methods, which didn't seem to be a priority during a pandemic.

Designing the dashboard

Initially I kept the design of the dashboard very simple, partly to build my own confidence and partly to keep the dashboard focused on answering the data query, and I worked hard to avoid cluttering it up (remembering that less is more!).

The first few visualisations I created concerned the number of bookings made per day and per timeslot and the number of bookings per school. These were relatively straightforward to create and instantly showed which library was the busiest, what the most popular timeslots were and which schools were the biggest users. I selected a line graph, a histogram and a bar chart for each element respectively. Although Power BI can create all kinds of wonderful graphs, I chose graphs that I thought would be well understood and interpreted by my audience, each of which conveyed its meaning effectively.

Figure 14.3 opposite shows the first draft of our new activity dashboard.

Using the dashboard

We launched the version of the dashboard shown in Figure 14.3 in time for Semester 1 (Sep–Dec 2020) as a trial. This gave managers the opportunity to familiarise themselves with the information that it contained and also to make some adjustments and additions based on their feedback.

However, the dashboards really came into their own during Semester 2 (January–May 2021) when we experienced some real highs and lows of demand for library spaces, which coincided with some of the worst infection

HOW DATA VISUALISATION TECHNIQUES INFORMED SERVICE DELIVERY   163

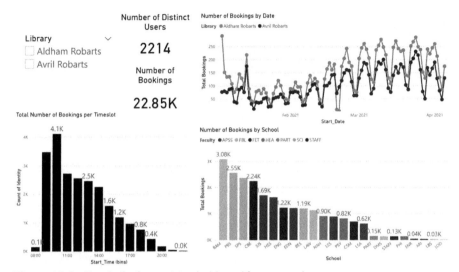

Figure 14.3 *First draft of an activity dashboard for case study*

rates of the pandemic and the beginnings of the UK lockdown easing. The biggest fluctuations in demand occurred during this semester: at the start of term, demand was very low, and our analyses showed that demand was concentrated among a small group of students who frequently used their full quota of booking allocations. As a result, we lifted the restrictions on the number of bookings students could make a week.

As time went on, however, and demand increased, we noticed we were getting more and more complaints that students were unable to make bookings because libraries were fully booked. Our ability to review our data gave us a better understanding of the nature of students' complaints. By comparing the booking data with our gate counts we found that we had a significant number of 'no shows' and that several students booked for long periods but actually only arrived quite late on in their booking slot. In response, we reintroduced quotas for students and restricted the duration of bookings that they could make. We noticed the complaints dropped significantly and although there were still some issues with demand, we were able to manage student expectations better.

Reflections

This case study has been a good chance to reflect on our approach to using data visualisation software to guide decision making in libraries and the good, bad and ugly of our experiences.

Let's start with the positives! One of the best things about using the data visualisation software to present the data was the instant results it can give you. Once you have set up your dashboard, you just refresh it whenever you have more data and it instantly gives you up-to-date analyses. This is a big improvement on any graphs that you create in Excel, which you have to update yourself. When you need real-time information (or very close to real-time information) this is the perfect approach.

Another advantage is the extent to which data visualisation software can be customised. Users can pick their own parameters and the visuals will interact accordingly. Again, this saves the analyst (me!) from having to produce numerous visuals all with a slightly different angle.

On the more negative side, data visualisation software requires a decent level of confidence in working with data. When setting it up you need to be able to structure and format your data in such a way that it will work with a complex system. I was fortunate that my workplace paid for me to complete a high-level data course during 2020, which helped no end. If you are serious about wanting to work with data better, it's worth investing in upskilling your staff in this area (and if any decision makers are reading this then please, please, invest in these skills!).

Another limitation for us was our inability to share the fully interactive reports with all staff. Because of licence restrictions (end-users need a Power BI licence in order to view the reports), I often had to share the reports as flat PDFs, which took away their interactive functionality.

And now, the ugly. The amount of time that we have to spend data cleaning is more than I would care to admit, given that I've been harking on about the advantages of a more automated approach. Even the data that is automatically generated by systems still requires reformatting, checking and restructuring to get it to work. Although the steps of the toolkit set out in this book are fantastic, sadly, sometimes they can be aspirational and in real life there's still a lot more messing with spreadsheets than anyone would like.

Final thoughts

A final couple of reflections from me. First, in order to get the most from using data-driven decision making, I suggest you develop a good relationship with your end-users. Collaborate with them to design a dashboard that suits their data needs. Consult them at each stage of the design process and get their feedback on any prototypes. Spend some time teaching them to use the dashboard, particularly if you are using a tool like Power BI to enable them to use the interactive tools confidently. This will help them get the most out of what you have built.

Also, be prepared to keep shouting about what you have done and advocate your work with senior managers as much as you can. I'm fortunate that in my role I attend our library leadership team meetings and therefore am in a position to bring regular snapshots from our live dashboard to meetings, which keeps them in managers' minds. If you are not in the same position, I strongly recommend that you find an advocate among those who are there. On the back of this continued advocacy, other managers have approached me about working on some of their data too. In addition, our director has been able to use my reports more widely when communicating with senior stakeholders, where they have been very well received.

My other reflection is to start small and start simple and build up from there. That's exactly what I did when creating the dashboard described above. I started with our Resource Booker data, and a few simple graphs depicting the number of bookings per day, a breakdown of schools and a breakdown of bookings by time. Over time, we added metrics for the number of bookings per student, headcount data and demographic data. When we started this approach all those different analyses would have been too overwhelming, but we have been able to build by starting with the basics.

Others' perspectives

You don't just need to take my word for it. When writing this, I spoke to some of our main decision makers, including our director, associate director and head of library engagement team, to ask for their perspectives on our use of data visualisation techniques. These are some of their comments:

- *Director* Our director observed that one of the key benefits of using data visualisation techniques was the ability to better understand who was using the library. Although we weren't always experiencing high demand, analysis of our demographic data showed that a very high percentage of library users were in the widening access participation groups. We were very aware that for many of our students, access to IT and/or suitable spaces to study was essential if they were to continue their studies successfully. By understanding the importance of providing spaces or IT for these students, they were better able to advocate to keep the libraries open.
- *Associate Director* One of the best aspects of using data visualisation techniques for our associate director was the level of insight that the

166   DATA-DRIVEN DECISIONS

analyses provided them. It really helped understand and address what the true issues were. For example, we were getting a lot of feedback from students who weren't able to book spaces as the library was always fully booked. As they had the data to hand they knew that the library wasn't always fully booked, suggesting students had difficulty in navigating the Resource Booker system. As a result we concentrated efforts on improving the instructions for booking, which reduced the number of complaints, rather than trying to create more spaces or manage demand.

- *Library engagement manager* Much as the library engagement manager appreciated how data visualisation techniques helped inform operations, such as staffing levels, opening hours and services, for them one of its most valuable impacts was in helping to explain to staff why it was important for the libraries to be open during the pandemic. Staff were understandably anxious about returning to site, but having those analyses to hand demonstrated to them why the library was deemed an essential service and the detrimental impact that the library being closed would have on the students. The analyses created a more relatable scenario for our staff and as the library engagement manager said, 'The data speaks louder than government guidance.'

Plans for the future

What's next for us? Well, we're going to keep on developing our current library activity report. This is particularly important for us as we are due to open a new learning commons area in June 2021. This new space is part of a wider shared building and also a new venture, therefore access to good, quick data will be essential to evaluating operations.

We also want to roll out the use of data visualisation techniques to some of our other areas of library activity, starting with our academic skills provision. We'd like to understand who is engaging with our academic skills sessions (and crucially who isn't!). This is a growing area for Library Services and the need for good quality data is essential as we develop.

I'd also like to explore some of our data collection methods to see if we can automate more of our data collection or storage to reduce the time we spend cleaning data. Chapter 4 stresses the importance of directly inputting your data rather than duplicating effort and there are a few areas where we could benefit from this.

I would also like to conduct some more qualitative analyses to better understand our students' experiences. Quantitative analysis can tell you the 'what' of a situation but it's the qualitative research that often unearths the 'why'. Qualitative responses are essential for understanding students' emotional journeys and often provide insights over and above what the quantitative can tell you. Although graphs and analyses are excellent for presenting factual data, I often find that a well-chosen quote is what truly resonates with people and sticks with them longer than blunt numbers do.

Finally, we're coming to the end of a strategic planning period so it's a good chance to use our data to review our progress over the last five years and evidence how we've developed, grown and changed. With this approach, I'm confident that our culture will become ever more dependent on data and evidence to make decisions, with successful results.

Appendix

Table A.1 *Blank table to use to identify data needs and related data queries, data sources, time frames and frequency*

Need	Data query	Data source	Time frames	Frequency

170 DATA-DRIVEN DECISIONS

Table A.2 *Blank manual data collection plan*

	Data source	Timeframe	Frequency
Proposed collection method			
Specifics (where, what, how, what is included and excluded, etc.)			
How data is stored			
How data is input			
Potential issues and risks			
Resources required			
Process what overlap or have potential to combine			

Bibliography

Adie, E. (2016) The Rise of Altmetrics. In Tattersall, A. (ed.), *Altmetrics: A Practical Guide for Librarians, Researchers and Academics*, Facet Publishing, 67–82.

Ahmed, W. (2017) Using Twitter as a Data Source: An Overview of Social Media Research Tools, https://blogs.lse.ac.uk/impactofsocialsciences/2017/05/08/using-twitter-as-a-data-source-an-overview-of-social-media-research-tools-updated-for-2017.

Allan, B. (2019) *The No-Nonsense Guide to Leadership, Management and Teamwork*, Facet Publishing.

Batrinca, B. and Treleaven, P. (2015) Social Media Analytics: A Survey of Techniques, Tools and Platforms, *AI & Society*, **30**, 89–116, https://doi.org/10.1007/s00146-014-0549-4.

Bladt, J., and Filbin, B. (2014) Who's Afraid of data-driven Management, *Harvard Business Review*, 16 May, https://hbr.org/2014/05/whos-afraid-of-data-driven-management.

Bradley, P. (2015) *Social Media for Creative Libraries*, 2nd edn, Facet Publishing.

Braun, V. and Clarke, V. (2006) Using Thematic Analysis in Psychology, *Qualitative Research in Psychology*, **3**, 77–101.

Burns, J. M. (1978) *Leadership*, Harper and Row.

Campbell Galman, S. (2016) *The Good, the Bad and The Data: Shane the Lone Ethnographer's Guide to Qualitative Data Analysis*, Taylor & Francis.

Cervone, H. F. (2017) Evaluating Social Media Presence: A Practical Application of Big Data and Analytics in Information Organizations, *Digital Library Perspectives*, **33** (1), 2–7

Cervone, H. F. (2018) Managing Data and Data Analysis in Information Organisations. In Hirsh, S. (ed.), *Information Services Today: An Introduction*, Rowman and Littlefield, 314–30

Crawford, K. (2018) Design Thinking Toolkit, Activity 16 – How Might We…?, https://spin.atomicobject.com/2018/12/12/how-might-we-design-thinking.

172 DATA-DRIVEN DECISIONS

Dam, R. F. and Siang, T. Y. (2020) Define and Frame Your Design Challenge by Creating Your Point Of View and Ask 'How Might We', www.interaction-design.org/literature/article/define-and-frame-your-design-challenge-by-creating-your-point-of-view-and-ask-how-might-we.

Dryden, A. (2014) Libraries and Marketing with Technology. In Thomsett-Scott, B. (ed.), *Marketing with Social Media*, Facet Publishing, 1–24.

Hicks, A. (2014) Digital Marketing in an Outreach Context. In Mackenzie, A. and Martin, L., *Mastering Digital Librarianship: Strategy, Networking and Discovery in Academic Libraries*, Facet Publishing, 3–22.

Investopedia (2021) A Review of Past Recessions, www.investopedia.com/articles/economics/08/past-recessions.asp.

OED Online (2021a) Oxford University Press, www.oed.com/view/Entry/38312?redirectedFrom=conclusion [subscription required].

OED Online (2021b) Oxford University Press, www.oed.com/view/Entry/205544 [subscription required].

Patel, M. B. and Vyas, P. R. (2019) Libraries and Social Media: Modern Practices and Coming Opportunities, *International Journal of Information Dissemination and Technology*, **9** (3), 129–31.

Phillips, D. and Brzozowska-Szczecina, E. (2020) Love at First Sight: Consolidating First Impressions. In Priestner, A. (ed.) *User Experience in Libraries, Yearbook 2019*, 123–8.

Pinfield, S., Cox, A. M. and Rutter, S. (2017) *Mapping the Future of Academic Libraries: A Report for* SCONUL, Society of College, National and University Libraries, www.sconul.ac.uk/sites/default/files/documents/SCONUL%20Report%20Mappi ng%20the%20Future%20of%20Academic%20Libraries.pdf.

Potter, N. (2012) *The Library Marketing Toolkit*, Facet Publishing

Priem, J. (2014) Altmetrics. In Cronin, B. and Sugimoto, C., *Beyond Bibliometrics: Harnessing Multidimensional Indicators of Scholarly Impact*, MIT Press, 263–87.

Priestner, A. (2018a) Affinity Mapping – Bringing Your Research Alive, *Information Professional*, www.cilip.org.uk/news/422225/Affinity-mapping-bringing-your-research-alive.htm.

Priestner, A. (2018b) The Value of Silence, *Information Professional*, www.cilip.org.uk/news/news.asp?id=422232.

Priestner, A. (2018c) UX in Libraries: Cognitive Maps, *Information Professional*, www.cilip.org.uk/general/custom.asp?page=CognitiveMapsMember.

Priestner, A. (2020) Barriers to User Experience Design. In Priestner, A. (ed.), *User Experience in Libraries, Yearbook 2019*, 1–10, UX in Libraries.

BIBLIOGRAPHY 173

Pshock, D. (2020) Reports Are Boring and You Know It. In Priestner, A. (ed.), *User Experience in Libraries Yearbook 2019*, 123–8, UX in Libraries.

Schmidt, A. and Etches, A. (2014) *Useful, Usable, Desirable: Applying User Experience Design to Your Library*, American Library Association.

Showers, B. (2015) Introduction: Getting the Measure of Analytics and Metrics. In Showers, B. (ed.), *Library Analytics and Metrics: Using Data to Drive Decisions and Services*, Facet Publishing, xxv–xxxi.

Showers, B. (2016) The Evolution of Library Metrics. In Tattersall, A. (ed.), *Altmetrics: A Practical Guide for Librarians, Researchers and Academics*, Facet Publishing, 49–65.

Stuart, D. (2015) Case Study 5.1: The Web Impact of Cultural Heritage Institutions. In Showers, B. (ed.), *Library Analytics and Metrics: Using Data to Drive Decisions and Services*, Facet Publishing, 117–36.

Sundt, A. and Davis, E. (2017) User Personas as a Shared Lens for Library UX, *Weave: Journal of Library User Experience*, **1** (6), 1–23.

Tattersall, A. (2016) Resources and Tools. In Tattersall, A. (ed.), *Altmetrics: A Practical Guide for Librarians, Researchers and Academics*, Facet Publishing, 109–36.

Taylor & Francis (2014) Use of Social Media by the Library: Current Practices and Future Opportunities, https://librarianresources.taylorandfrancis.com/insights/library-advocacy/use-social-media-by-the-library.

UK Data Service (2021) Consent for Data Sharing, www.ukdataservice.ac.uk/manage-data/legal-ethical/consent-data-sharing/inform-participants.aspx.

UoW (2021) Student Experience Committee, University of Westminster, www.westminster.ac.uk/about-us/our-university/corporate-information/governance-and-structure/academic-council/student-experience-committee.

Winn, D., Rivosecchi, M., Bjerke, J. and Groenendyk, M. (2017) MTL 2.0: A Report on the Social Media Usage and User Engagement of the 'Big Four' Academic Libraries in Montreal, *Journal of Academic Librarianship*, **43**, 297–304.

Index

actioning 69–75
  case study 95–6, 149–52
  feedback 70, 74
  planning actions 73–5
  report writing 70–2
  sharing data 70–2
  UoW case study 149–52
affinity mapping 121–2
age, collection 102
alternative data sources 127–40
  see also social media
altmetrics, social media 136–7
analysis 57–68
  see also conclusions
  affinity mapping 121–2
  altmetrics 136–7
  anomalies 59–60
  ATLAS software 121
  averaging data 58–9
  coding 120
  conclusions 62–8
  context of your data 59–62
  data mining 134–5
  data visualisation 161–2
  dedicated software 121
  deductive vs inductive analysis 119
  Excel 120–1, 160–1
  free text analysis 119–21
  Google Analytics 138–9
  Google Trends 139
  inductive vs deductive analysis 119
  massaging data 57–9

maths 120
NVivo software 121
outcomes measurement and
  evaluation 134–5
Post-it Notes 122
prejudging data 62–3
representing data correctly 62
software 121–2
spreadsheets 120–1, 160–1
transcribing 119–20
UoW case study 147–9
usage data 129–34
user engagement data and dialogue
  134–5
user experience (UX) 119–22
visual analysis 120–1
web-based analytics 137–9
anonymising data 117
ATLAS software 121
author's background 3–4
automated data collection 36–8
  saving data 37–8
  sorting data 37
  timeframes 36–7

behavioural mapping, UX technique
  116
benchmarking, collection mapping 100
book layout 9–10
  chapter layout 10
Bradley, Phil 128

176 DATA DRIVEN DECISIONS

case study 90–6
  actioning 95–6, 149–52
  background 90–1
  balance of work within the liaison team 91–2
  conclusion 96
  data collected 91–2
  data culture 141–53
  data inferences 92–5
  discussions 95–6
  identifying the roles in the team 94
  non-core liaison work 93–4
  process reviews 95–6
  review 96
  University of Westminster (UoW) 141–53
categorising collections 105–6
choosing your data 23–6
coding, translating data 47
coding for analysis 120
cognitive mapping, UX technique 109–10
collecting data *see* data collection
collection age 102
collection content 99
collection mapping 97–106
  see also mapping data
  benchmarking 100
  categorising your collection 105–6
  collection age 102
  collection content 99
  collection spend 104–5
  collection strengths and weaknesses 99–100
  collection uses 103–4
  comparing collections 100
  Dewey area mapping 101, 102, 103–4
  planning 98–9
  rarity and uniqueness of your collection 100
  research and teaching needs 100–2
  Research Excellence Framework (REF) 101
  Royal Holloway Library 105–6
  understanding your collection as a concept 97–8
  understand your collection 99

collection spend 104–5
collection strengths and weaknesses 99–100
collection uses 103–4
combining methods, manual data collection 34–5
comparable data *see* normalising data
comparing collections 100
compassionate data-driven service 89–90
compiling data, UoW case study 147
conclusions 62–8
  see also analysis
  case study 96
  checking conclusions 67–8
  drawing conclusions 66–7
  exploratory conclusions 68
  patterns 63–5
  surprises 63, 66
  trends 63–6
  UoW case study 149–52
context in the information profession 4–5
COVID-19 recession 5
cultural probes, UX technique 114–15
customer services, social media 135–6

dashboard, data visualisation 158, 159, 161–5
data champions 87
data collection 23–38
  see also automated data collection; manual data collection
  blank table 169
  case study 91–2
  efficiency and effectiveness 79–80
  feedback 29–30
  frequency 26, 27
  planning 23–4, 27–9
  review 79–80
  timeframes 24–6, 27
data culture, UoW case study 141–53
data inferences, case study 92–5
data-led culture 86–9
  data champions 87
  identifying data personalities in the team 87–9

data mining, social media 134–5
data needs 15–17, 19, 21–2, 27
  blank table 169
  UoW case study 143–5
data patterns 63–5
data queries 16–17, 19–22, 27
data sources 17–22, 27
  identifying data sources 19–20
  qualitative data 18–19, 20
  quantitative data 17–19, 20
data storage 30
  review 80
data surprises 63, 66
data trends 63–6
data types 17–20
data visualisation 48–53
  analysis 161–2
  commandments 49–52
  dashboard 158, 159, 161–5
  displaying data 48–9
  Liverpool John Moores University
    (LJMU) 155–67
  others' perspectives 165–6
  patterns 162
  Piktochart tool 156–7
  plans for the future 166–7
  Power BI tool 158–9
  reflection 163–4
  Resource Booker tool 160
  VLOOKUP function in Excel 160–1
data with compassion 89–90
dates and times, normalising
    (comparable) data 41–4
dedicated software for analysis 121
deductive vs inductive analysis 119
Dewey area mapping 101, 102, 103–4
direct input, manual data collection 35
discussions, case study 95–6
displaying data, data visualisation 48–9
driver for change, UoW case study 142

effective data 79
efficiency and effectiveness, data
    collection 79–80
embedding manual data collection
    33–4
embedding new proceses 82

embedding the new model, UoW case
    study 152
ethics of research
  UK Data Service 117
  user experience (UX) 117–18
Excel for analysis 120–1, 160–1
  see also spreadsheets

feedback
  actioning 70, 74
  data collection 29–30
  review 78, 79
financial challenges 4–5
focus groups, UX technique 114
FRAMES model, report writing 123–4
free text analysis 119–20
fresh eye approach 20
full-time equivalent (FTE), normalising
    (comparable) data 45–6

Gantt charts 74, 75
Google Analytics 138–9
Google Trends 139
graffiti wall, UX technique 116

hours in a working day, normalising
    (comparable) data 44–5

identifying data personalities in the
    team 87–9
inductive vs deductive analysis 119
interviews, UX technique 113–14

Jisc Library Hub Compare tool 100

leading with data 85–9
lessons learned, UoW case study 152–3
Liverpool John Moores University
    (LJMU) 155–67
  see also data visualisation
love or break-up letters, UX technique
    116

manual data collection 28–36
  blank table 169
  combining methods 34–5
  data storage 30

178 DATA DRIVEN DECISIONS

direct input 35
embedding manual data collection
  33–4
organising data 30–3
planning 28–9, 34–6
saving data 35
spreadsheets 30–3, 35, 37–8
staff input and trials 29–30
start collecting data 28–9
top tips 34–6
mapping data 39–55
  see also collection mapping
  creating a map of your data 52–5
  data visualisation 48–52
  importance 39–40
  normalising (comparable) data 40–8
  updating your map 55
marketing activity, social media
  130–4
marketing cycle, social media 131–2,
  134
market research, social media 132–4
maths for analysis 120

needs, data *see* data needs
normalising (comparable) data 40–8
  dates and times 41–4
  full-time equivalent (FTE) 45–6
  hours in a working day 44–5
  qualitative data, translating 46–7
  staffing 45–6
  time-logged vs non-time-logged
    data 45
  translating data 46–8
  weekday or weekend? 44
NVivo software 121

observations, UX technique 111–12
organising data 30–3
original data, UoW case study 142
outcomes measurement and evaluation,
  social media 134–5
overnight opening, UoW case study
  143–53

palatable and understandable data,
  report writing 71

patterns
  data 63–5
  data visualisation 162
  UoW case study 148–9
Piktochart, data visualisation tool 156–7
planning
  actions 73–5
  collection mapping 98–9
  data collection 23–4, 27–9, 34–6
  manual data collection 28–9, 34–6
  project 73–5
Post-it Notes for analysis 122
Power BI, data visualisation tool 158–9
practising 21–2
prejudging data 62–3
process reviews, case study 95–6
project planning 73–5
  Gantt charts 74, 75

qualitative data 18–19, 20
  coding 47
  normalising (comparable) data 46–7
  tidying 48
  UoW case study 146–7
quantitative data 17–19, 20
  UoW case study 146
queries, data *see* data queries

rarity and uniqueness of your collection
  100
reasons for data-driven decisions 6
recession effects on the information
  profession 4–5
recruiting participants, user experience
  (UX) 118–19
REF (Research Excellence Framework)
  101
reflection
  data visualisation 163–4
  UoW case study 152–3
report writing
  FRAMES model 122–3
  layout 72
  length 72
  palatable and understandable data
    71
  purpose 71

INDEX 179

user experience (UX) 122–3
research, user experience *see* user
  experience research
research and teaching needs 100–2
research ethics 117–18
Research Excellence Framework (REF)
  101
research problems, user experience (UX)
  124
Resource Booker, data visualisation tool
  160
responses to financial challenges 5
review 77–82
  case study 96
  data collection 79–80
  data storage 80
  effective data 79
  embedding new processes 82
  feedback 78, 79
  how to review 78–80
  impact of changes 80–1
  making changes 80–2
  questions to explore 78–80
  reasons for 77–8
  story of your data 81
  trialling approaches 81
Royal Holloway Library, collection
  mapping 105–6

saving data
  automated data collection 37–8
  manual data collection 35
service improvements, social media
  135–6
social media 127–40
  altmetrics 136–7
  background 129
  Bradley, Phil 128
  customer services 135–6
  data from social media marketing
    activity 130–4
  data mining 134–5
  Google Analytics 138–9
  Google Trends 139
  libraries and 128–9
  marketing activity 130–4
  marketing cycle 131–2, 134

market research 132–4
outcomes measurement and
  evaluation 134–5
service improvements 135–6
terminology 129
usage data 129–34
user engagement data and dialogue
  134–5
uses 128–30
web-based analytics 137–9
software for analysis 121
sorting data
  automated data collection 37
  translating data 47–8
sources of data *see* data sources
spend, collection 104–5
spreadsheets
  analysis 120–1, 160–1
  Excel for analysis 120–1, 160–1
  graphs 49
  layouts 144–6, 158, 160–1
  manual data collection 30–3, 35, 37–8
staffing, normalising (comparable) data
  45–6
story of your data 81
surprises, data 63, 66

teaching and research needs 100–2
tidying data, translating data 48
  time-logged vs non-time-logged data,
    normalising (comparable) data
    45
timeframes
  automated data collection 36–7
  data collection 24–6, 27
toolkit 15–82
  benefits 7–8
  circular approach 11
  model 10–11
  overview 6–8
  using the toolkit 9–11
touchstone tours, UX technique 110–11
transactional vs transformational work
  86
transcribing for analysis 120
translating data
  coding 47

180 DATA DRIVEN DECISIONS

normalising (comparable) data 46–8
sorting data 47–8
tidying data 48
trends, data 63–6
trialling approaches 81

UK Data Service 117
understand your collection 99
University of Westminster (UoW)
141–53
actioning 149–52
analysis 147–9
compiling data 147
conclusions 149–52
data culture 141–53
data needs 143–5
driver for change 142
embedding the new model 152
lessons learned 152–3
original data 142
overnight opening case study 143–53
patterns 148–9
qualitative data, getting started 146–7
quantitative data, getting started 146
reflection 152–3
structure 141–2
usage data, social media 129–34
user engagement data and dialogue,
social media 134–5
user experience (UX) research 107–25
anonymising data 117

behavioural mapping 116
cognitive mapping 109–10
cultural probes 114–15
ethics of research 117–18
focus groups 113–14
graffiti wall 116
interviews 113–14
love or break-up letters 116
observations 111–12
recruiting participants 118–19
report writing 122–3
research problems 124
stages 108
techniques 108–16
touchstone tours 110
undertaking UX research in a library
108
web usability testing 111
uses, collection 103–4
UX *see* user experience research

visual analysis 120–1
visualisation, data *see* data visualisation
VLOOKUP function in Excel, data
visualisation 160–1

web-based analytics, social media 137–9
web usability testing, UX technique 111
weekday or weekend?, normalising
(comparable) data 44
writing up *see* report writing